For Justin Chearno

This book is a collection of stories centered around meals we shared with winemakers, where we talked not only about wine but also about food and life. No one felt more at home at these tables than our friend Justin Chearno, who spent the last two decades tasting, talking, and laughing with many of the winemakers featured in these pages. His generous ability to capture and share these moments brought natural wine to life for countless people who had the chance to cross his path. We dedicate this book to his memory.

SPILLED

SPILLED: NATURAL WINEMAKERS STORIES & RECIPES

Stephanie Mercier Voyer
Zev Rovine
David McMillan

Photography by Xavier Tera

New York · Paris · London · Milan

CONTENTS

TEXT

11 Introduction
13 How to Use This Book
15 What Is Natural Wine and Why Does It Matter?
17 A Glossary of Sorts
21 How Natural Wine Is Made
25 The Many Shades and Styles of Natural Wines

247 Further Readings
248 Acknowledgments
250 Index

REGIONS

FRANCE

32 A Brief History of Natural Wine in France
35 The Loire
55 The Jura
74 Burgundy
125 Auvergne
140 The Rhône
163 The Languedoc

ITALY

172 A Brief History of Natural Wine in Italy
174 Friuli Venezia Giulia
183 Trentino–Alto Adige
191 Emilia-Romagna
199 The Veneto
206 Tuscany
215 Lazio
220 Sicily

WINERIES

FRANCE

37	DOMAINE DE L'ANGE VIN Jean-Pierre & Noëlla Robinot
49	DOMAINE TESSIER Simon & Philippe Tessier
56	MAISON MAENAD Katie Worobeck
65	DOMAINE DES MIROIRS Kenjiro & Mayumi Kagami
78	CHÂTEAU DE BÉRU Athénaïs de Béru
87	DOMAINE LES FAVERELLES Patrick Bringer & Isabelle Georgelin
92	Marthe Henry
100	DOMAINE CHANDON DE BRIAILLES François & Claude de Nicolay
106	MAISON EN BELLES LIES Pierre & Michèle Fenals
114	MAISON VALETTE Philippe & Cécile Valette
126	DOMAINE LA BOHÈME Patrick Bouju & Justine Loiseau
134	Marie & Vincent Tricot
142	Lolita Sene
149	Anders Frederik Steen & Anne Bruun Blauert
156	LES DEUX TERRES Vincent Fargier & Manu Cunin
164	Charlotte & Jean-Baptiste Sénat

ITALY

176	Dario Prinčič
184	AZIENDA AGRICOLA FORADORI Elisabetta Foradori
192	SEBASTIAN VAN DE SYPE WINERY Sebastian & Marieke Van de Sype
200	SASSARA VINI Alessia & Stefano Bertaiola
208	LA GINESTRA Dario Nocci, Matteo Rinaldi & Co.
216	ABBIA NÒVA Pierluca & Daniele Proietti
222	Frank Cornelissen
231	CANTINA MARILINA Marilina Paternò
238	AZIENDA AGRICOLA SERRAGGHIA Gabrio, Geneviève & Giotto Bini

RECIPES

FRANCE

44	Endive Salad with Boiled Eggs
46	French Veal Stew
52	Beer-Braised Rabbit with Prunes
60	Roast Chicken with Morels and Vin Jaune
62	Salad with Pea Vinaigrette
70	Carrot Salad with Lentils, Shiso, and Sesame Seeds
72	Nikujaga with Yuzu Kosho
84	Whole Roasted Harvest Fish
90	Quiche Lorraine with Wild Mushrooms
96	Gaston Gérard Chicken
98	Grandmother's Crème Caramel
104	Boeuf Bourguignon
110	Slow-Cooked Pork with White Wine and Root Vegetables
112	Fresh Plum Tart
120	Mâconnais Onion Soup
122	Île Flottante
130	Braised Lamb Shank with Spelt
132	Wine Beets and Citrus
138	Baking Sheet Pear Tart
146	Kabyle Couscous with Lamb
152	Wild Mushroom Risotto
154	Broccolini with Preserved Lemons
160	Caillettes
168	Late Summer Stuffed Garden Vegetables

ITALY

180	Rabbit Biechi
188	Zucchini Soup with Fresh Cheese
196	Osso Bucco
204	Bollito Misto with Pearà Sauce
212	Tagliatelle with Zucchini and Gorgonzola
218	Baked Porcini and Fig Salad
228	Tempura Artichoke Hearts
234	Zucchini Leaf Soup
236	Fried Bread with Eggs
244	Panelle with Spicy Caper Condiment

Introduction

BY STEPHANIE MERCIER VOYER

When people ask me why I love natural wine, my answer usually turns into a story—and that story is never really about wine.

I first came into contact with natural wine in my early twenties after I got hired as a server at Nora Gray, a fantastic Italian restaurant in Montreal. To say that my wine knowledge at the time was nonexistent would be quite the understatement. In the lead up to my first day, I tried as hard as I could to educate myself, using books and the internet, but I always wound up feeling overwhelmed and, quite frankly, really bored.

That all changed when Ryan Gray, one of the restaurant's owners and sommelier, first walked me through his wine list—a thoughtful collection of some of France's and Italy's best natural-wine producers. Instead of trying to drill down facts about each wine, which I would have instantly forgotten, Ryan told me stories about the winemakers whose work he admired. It clicked.

While wine books had left me scrambling to stay awake, wondering if I'd ever care enough to memorize all ten Beaujolais crus, natural wine arrived with a built-in narrative that featured characters I could root for, heck, even fall for. Some lived in castles and others in houses fit for fairies. Some had rugged hands the size of bear paws, while others were dainty and wrote beautiful prose. Some had abandoned successful careers in cities, while others had left an entire country behind. Slowly, a picture emerged. There they were, a group of outcasts and underdogs who had chosen to fight against an oppressive and destructive system, and do things the hard way, naturally.

After that, learning about viticultural practices, winemaking history, and regulations came easily because it colored the stories of winemakers I now had grown attached to. I grew obsessed with learning everything I could about the winemakers who crafted the wines I loved. I talked to industry friends, read firsthand accounts posted on WordPress blogs by wine writers and importers, interviewed winemakers for magazines, and sometimes even visited them myself. I loved being able to share what I'd learned with guests, and I reveled at the moment when I'd notice a flicker in their eyes, indicating that they, too, were hooked.

In the winter of 2018, David and I found ourselves fighting seasonal depression by meeting every morning for coffee and swapping stories about restaurants and winemakers, but mostly about the tragic comedy of our dating lives. When he suggested we should collaborate on a cookbook about natural wine, and proposed that we team up with Zev, I did not hesitate. I said yes.

Before our paths converged, David, Zev, and I each found ourselves drawn to the world of natural wine in our own ways. Before building and leaving the Joe Beef empire to become a farmer and winemaker in the Quebec countryside, David came up as a young chef, enthralled with the world of classical French cuisine and wine. However, over the last decade or so, his once fierce love of Burgundy morphed into a burning desire to drink wines that matched his approach to food. During one of those early conversations, he told me, "It's not about appellations and labels; it's about relationships." As

1. (Left) David and Steph laugh with Zev, who is standing off-frame, during a visit to Hayfield Farm, David's farm and vineyard in St-Armand, Quebec.

a chef and restaurateur, David prided himself on building relationships with small farmers, butchers, mushroom guys, and cheesemongers. Natural wine allowed him the same opportunity.

Zev's journey to becoming one of the country's biggest natural-wine importers is so convoluted—involving a stint on Rikers Island and a simple contest that changed the course of his life—it deserves its own book. In any case, in 2007, with next to no money, he launched the eponymous Zev Rovine Selections (ZRS), an importation company specializing in natural wine. At the time, Zev couldn't afford to constantly travel to France to meet new winemakers, so instead, he started taking regular trips to Montreal to explore the city's natural-wine scene, which was eons ahead of New York's. "I'd write down the names of winemakers I'd see on wine lists," he recalls. "Once I got back home, I would call them all, book a trip, and I'd do my best to convince them to work with me." Over the next decade, Zev grew his company by building meaningful relationships and friendships with natural winemakers around the world.

From the start, we knew we didn't want to write a serious wine book, the kind that's unapproachable, dense, and gathers dust on a shelf. If you want to take a deep dive into yields, crops, and fermentation times, this is not the book for you.

We set out to write the kind of book we would have wanted to read when we first discovered natural wine—a book that is intimate yet informative, filled with personal stories, evocative photography, and recipes that make you feel like you're sitting at the table with us. To do that, we had to get up close and personal with the vignerons at the forefront of the natural-wine movement. And so, we hit the road.

Accompanied by our friend and longtime collaborator Xavier Tera, who so brilliantly captured the dreamy and raw spirit of this odd community, we decided to focus our journey on the two countries that made us fall in love with natural wine: France and Italy. We drove countless hours through the French and Italian countrysides, slept on the floor of an overbooked hotel, spent sleepless nights in a haunted castle, picked hundreds of grapes, crushed a thousand more, got into fights, sang at the top of our lungs, and laughed uncontrollably. But every day, no matter what, we wound up sitting around a dinner table with winemakers, spilling both our wine and our secrets.

Throughout that process, I found out that, yes, wine can be intimidating and tedious. But that behind every great wine, there is a great human story anyone can relate to. While about wine on the surface, the stories in these pages explore themes we all have to contend with like patience, regrets, death, greed, and legacy. It's what makes us human—and it's what makes me love natural wine.

We don't expect this book to make you want to become a natural winemaker. Or to even buy wine from every producer mentioned in these pages (although you should try to taste as many of their wines as you can because the love and work that goes into each one is palpable). But maybe you'll cook Noëlla Robinot's French Veal Stew the same way she makes it for visitors returning from a long day in the cellar with her husband, the winemaker Jean-Pierre Robinot. Or make Marie and Vincent Tricot's baking sheet pear tart for your friends before an impromptu dance party erupts in your living room like it did during our visit. Or maybe you'll prepare a big batch of Elisabetta Foradori's simple soup with the season's first zucchini.

We hope you pick up this book to cook for your loved ones, and perhaps as you open a bottle of wine and start sharing a story you read about, you, too, will notice a flicker in their eyes.

How to Use This Book

In the years we spent writing this book, I don't think we ever figured out a straightforward way to explain it to people. "Is it a wine book?" Sort of, but it's also a cookbook. "Oh, so it's food and wine pairings?" Definitely not! "What is it, then?" We eventually landed on a description that became the tagline for this book: natural winemakers stories and recipes. *Spilled* is a cross between a wine book and a cookbook, with a great deal of storytelling in the mix, and because of that, it means there are lots of different ways to use it.

You can use it as decor. Of course, we'd love it if you at least opened it once just to flip through the pages and perhaps even read a few words (after all, we did spend years of our lives working on it). But we get it, books are for nerds. That's why we tasked our friends at Perron-Roettinger with creating a cover so special, this book could ascend to object-dom.

You can use it as a photo book. If you've managed to open the book, but still feel like the essays and profiles are a bit daunting, you're in luck. Shot on film, Xavier's evocative photographs are not only beautiful and textured, but they also perfectly capture the spirit of our journey, along with the people and places we visited. To give the images a bit more context, we wrote short captions, sometimes insightful, other times stupid, depending on whether we could remember where or when a photo was taken. (In our defense, our research involved a lot of wine drinking.)

You can use it to learn about natural wine... or whatever. If it was only up to us, every page of this book would come with a disclaimer that this is not a serious wine book. While we do include some basic information about natural wine and how it's made at the beginning of this book, along with other historical tidbits throughout, *Spilled* is by no means a textbook, encyclopedia, or atlas of natural wine. We deliberately chose not to include any maps in the entire book. Partly because we barely cover half of France's and Italy's winemaking regions, but mostly because we use Google maps to get literally anywhere, sometimes to a fault (like that time we drove two hours in the wrong direction to a different location Google had marked as La Ginestra). That said we enlisted our talented friend Emilie Campbell, who also happens to be one of the most thoughtful wine professionals we know, to bring to life some of the more dense and technical portions of the book with illustrations. We do hope you learn a thing or two about natural wine within these pages, but if you are looking for a deeper dive, we've gathered a list of our favorite reads on p.247. Keep in mind that publishing a book is a rather slow process, which means that some of the information we included in these pages at the time of writing might be outdated by the time you read it. Think of the information in this book as a snapshot of a moment in time.

You can read it like a magazine. We don't expect anyone to read this book cover to cover in chronological order, which is why we organized the table of contents a little differently than most books. By grouping the different types of content together, we wanted to make it easier for you to find your way around the book, while also allowing you to pick a single piece to read depending on your mood. Perhaps you want to learn more about the history of a specific winemaking region like the Auvergne (p.125). Or maybe you're looking for some fun stories to share with your friends when you bring a bottle of Susucaru to the next dinner party (p.222). You can even use this book as some sort of wish list the next time you visit your local wine store or as a resource when you're planning out your next vacation.

You can use it as a cookbook. Despite not being able to fit every recipe we enjoyed in the company of some of our favorite winemakers, you will find thirty-four of our favorite dishes in these pages. In our selection we aimed to include a balanced mix for you to recreate at home, including meat, fish, and vegetable dishes, as well as a few desserts. The recipes are organized by winemaker, which are grouped by region and country. (They are also listed separately in the table of contents and broken down by ingredients in the index.)

The most important thing you need to keep in mind if you choose to cook from this book is that these recipes were, for the most part, not developed by professional chefs. These are homemade meals and family recipes prepared for us by home cooks who happen to be some of the world's best natural winemakers.

In writing these recipes, we tried to stay faithful to the original ingredients and instructions we were given—even though some of them left David speechless or prompted him to call Steph to rant about how the instructions made no sense and that "No professional chef would cook that way!" All that to say, we are aware that some instructions might seem a bit odd, especially for those of you who have a professional cooking background.

It's no secret that not all food is created equal, which is why David adapted each recipe to make it replicable in a North American home kitchen. Anyone who's ever tasted French butter will know nothing this side of the Atlantic remotely compares to its depth of flavor. Same goes for produce and meats: ingredients used by our winemaker friends in the French and Italian countryside won't be exactly the same as the ones you will find in supermarket chains across the US. (A lot of these differences are a result of different agricultural practices and regulations.) In any case, here are some ingredient pointers to help you cook from this book:

- Just like the wine, ingredients are organic (or as natural as possible)
- Fish is sustainably sourced
- Eggs are large
- Butter is salted unless otherwise specified
- Milk is whole
- Cream is heavy
- Olive oil is extra virgin (bonus point if it's made by a natural winemaker like Frank Cornelissen, Pacina, or La Villana)
- Salt is from the sea (we use flaky sea salt for finishing touches)
- Black pepper is freshly ground
- Parsley is flat-leaf

What Is Natural Wine and Why Does It Matter?

We would have loved to open this chapter with a punchy one-liner, something bold, like "natural wine is wine that holds nothing back," or "natural wine is wine that bears it all," which would have hopefully made you, the reader, feel like we *truly* got it. But none of them felt quite right. Probably because what these kinds of catchy statements fail to capture, and part of the reason natural wine continues to be hard to define, is that it is more than just a beverage—natural wine is also a culture.

The beverage itself is fairly easy to describe. Natural wine is wine made with grapes grown without the use of systemic chemicals and then fermented, aged, and bottled with no additives, except for the occasional dash of sulfites. While there is currently no legal designation for natural wine, various organizations, such as Nature et Progrès in France and VinNatur in Italy, provide some form of certification. Meanwhile, well-known certifications like Organic and Demeter mostly regulate farming practices, meaning both allow the use of additives during the winemaking process, except for commercial yeast addition in Demeter-certified wines. These caveats have resulted in confusion for consumers while providing fodder for critics to dismiss natural wine as a mere trend.

In many ways, the aversion to put natural wine in a (figurative) box is a byproduct of its culture. Natural wine was born out of a spirit of defiance and a refusal to conform, both to the chemical farming industry that took wine production by storm and to the growing consolidation and marketing movements that made wine more consistent, but also blander and more uniform.

Natural wine doesn't exist in a vacuum. It exists in opposition to conventional wine, which is why it is most often defined by what it isn't rather than what it is. In order to understand natural wine, its culture, and why natural winemakers, with their antiestablishment stance, have typically resisted codifying natural wine, we must understand the rise of conventional winemaking.

Natural wine is nothing new. It might be difficult for us to imagine a time before Monsanto and large-scale agriculture, but before the rise of industrialization beginning in the late nineteenth century, all wine was made naturally. Knowing what we now know about the environmental devastation brought by heavy machinery and chemical use, it's hard to understand how people bought into it. But it's important to remember that at the time, these technological advancements felt like miracles. Imagine being told that a machine or a treatment could allow you to grow your production and lift your family out of poverty? Or even better, get rich? You'd have no way of imagining that these changes would eventually result in dwindling wildlife populations and cities filled with smoke from uncontrollable wildfires. You'd probably just say, "Where do I sign?" That is what happened gradually over the course of more than a century. Each event and innovation led to another, enabling wineries to grow while slowly destroying our natural ecosystems, only to pump out standardized wine disconnected from its origins.

The phylloxera crisis of the late nineteenth century, which almost completely decimated European vineyards, led to the loss of vine diversity as growers favored replanting popular varietals over native ones. The early twentieth century welcomed the use of chemical fertilizers, sulfites, and electric presses. In 1935, the creation of France's AOC system put pressure on winemakers to plant varieties that were recognized under the newly established appellation system. In the 1950s, farmers embraced the use of tractors in favor of horses. Then, when the export market boomed a few years later, winemakers were encouraged to produce more wine to generate more profit. But in order to survive long journeys, the wine needed to be more stable. As a result, winemakers turned to more extreme filtration techniques and higher sulfite dosages. In the 1970s, harvesting machines were popularized and coincided with the invention of Monsanto's Roundup, a systemic herbicide cocktail, which made it possible to plant vines in inhospitable environments while generating higher yields and significantly reducing the need for manual labor.

By the 1980s, use of chemicals such as Roundup in vineyards had eradicated nearly all native yeast populations. Instead of taking a step back, winemakers were presented with a miracle solution: commercial yeast that could jumpstart any fermentation. During that same decade, wine critic Robert Parker's 100-point scoring system became so influential that sales for a highly rated wine would soar while the rest would tank. To capitalize on this, producers began to tailor their winemaking practices to match the critic's taste. This led to the homogenization of wine across the globe and an even greater embrace of additives used to tweak a wine's flavor profile.

The 1990s brought along even more technological advancements, with techniques like reverse-osmosis and micro-oxygenation that could be used to lower a wine's acidity and alcohol levels. Unfortunately the list goes on; this is by no means an exhaustive timeline of how we got to where we are today, just a drop in the barrel.

As a culture, natural wine makes an attempt to look back at how things were done before industrialization, in order to work in a way that is less harmful to the environment and to produce wines that are downright delicious. Is it harder? Of course it is. There are no shortcuts with natural wine, no get-rich-quick schemes. Natural winemakers can't hide behind chemicals, additives, and tech. They have to put in the work to produce wine that honors its terroir and bears it all: where it came from, how its grapes were farmed, how much rain or sun there was that year, and even who made it.

Why does any of it matter? Well, because natural wine encourages us to care. To care about the environment. About what we put in our bodies. About transparency. About providing jobs to real people instead of machines, a point made even more pertinent with the rise of artificial intelligence. What natural wine ultimately boils down to is caring about people.

By the end of this book, you will hopefully be more informed about natural wine, how and where it is made, who makes it, and what they like to eat. But, more importantly, we hope you fall in love with the people and the culture portrayed in these pages. We for sure have.

1. Swirling, sipping, and spitting during a tank sampling session with winemaker Romain Le Bars, who, after working under Tavel legend Eric Pfifferling from Domaine de L'Anglore, now makes fresh, fruit-forward wines in the Gard.

A Glossary of Sorts

The language of wine can make learning about the subject feel extremely daunting. To make it easier on all of us, we've created an inexhaustive list of wine terms you might encounter while reading this book.

Amphora: A traditional clay vessel used for fermenting and ageing wine since ancient Greek and Roman times.

Appellation: A legally defined and protected geographical indication used to identify where grapes for a wine were grown. The appellation can also regulate various aspects of wine production, including grape varietals, viticultural practices, and winemaking techniques.

Barrel: A cylindrical container, traditionally made of oak, used for fermenting and ageing wine. It influences the flavor, aroma, and texture of the wine.

Carbonic maceration: A winemaking technique where whole grapes ferment in a closed, carbon dioxide–rich environment before being crushed to produce fruit-forward wines with low tannins.

Cask: An ageing container similar to a barrel, but typically larger in size, that can be made of wood or stainless steel.

Chaptalization: The process of adding sugar to grape must before or during fermentation to increase the alcohol content of a finished wine. It was named after French chemist Jean-Antoine Chaptal, who popularized the technique in the early nineteenth century.

Cooperative: A group of winegrowers who pool their resources and grapes to produce wine collectively, sharing facilities and equipment.

Cru: A French vineyard recognized for producing exceptional-quality wine.

Cuvée: A specific blend or batch of wine.

Disgorgement: A process in sparkling wine production where the sediment from the secondary fermentation is removed from the bottle.

DOC: An Italian wine classification (like an appellation) used to indicate that a wine is produced in a specific region and adheres to strict regulations regarding its production.

Dosage: A mixture of sugar and reserved wine added to sparkling wine after disgorgement to balance acidity and achieve the desired sweetness level.

Egg: An egg-shaped fermentation vessel, typically made of concrete, which promotes natural circulation of the wine during fermentation.

Élevage: The process of maturing and refining a wine between fermentation and bottling, using techniques like barrel-ageing, stirring the lees, and managing oxygen exposure.

Filtration: The process of removing suspended particles from wine to clarify and stabilize it before bottling.

Fining agents: Substances that are added to wine to remove unwanted particles, improve clarity, and stabilize the wine. These include bentonite, egg whites, and gelatin.

Grape must: Freshly crushed grape juice that contains the skins, seeds, and stems.

Grape varietal: A specific type of grape, such as pinot noir or Sangiovese.

Indigenous or native grape varietal: A type of grape that is native to a specific region.

International grape varietal: A widely recognized type of grape, often of French origins, that is grown around the world.

Lees: The sediment consisting of dead yeast cells and other particles that settle at the bottom of a fermentation vessel.

Maceration: The process of soaking grape skins, seeds, and stems in the juice to extract color, flavor, and tannins. This is how red, rosé, and orange wines develop their color.

Minerality: A tasting term used to describe the subtle flavors and aromas in wine that resemble minerals, such as flint, chalk, or slate, often associated with the terroir.

Mouse: A tasting term and a wine fault that bears a distinctive off-flavor. For some people, the taste of mousy wine is reminiscent of a wet rag, peanuts, corn chips, and, of course, a mouse.

Négociants: Winemakers who buy grapes from various growers to produce wine under their own label.

Organoleptic: A term that refers to aspects experienced by the senses, including taste, smell, sight, and touch.

Oxidation: A chemical reaction that occurs when wine is exposed to oxygen. When a wine is oxidized, it means that it has been negatively affected by oxidation, resulting in off-flavors and browning. On the other hand, an oxidative wine is a wine that has been intentionally exposed to controlled amounts of oxygen to enhance complexity and develop desired characteristics, such as nutty, caramel, or sherry-like notes.

Paysan: A French term that refers to a small-scale winegrower or winemaker with a traditional approach.

Reduction: A tasting term referring to a wine fault caused by a lack of oxygen, resulting in off-aromas such as sulfur and rotten eggs.

Residual sugar: The amount of sugar remaining in wine after fermentation, contributing to the wine's sweetness.

Secondary fermentation: As the name suggests, a fermentation that occurs after the wine's initial fermentation. It is commonly used in sparkling winemaking to develop bubbles, either in the bottle or in a tank.

Sulfites, Sulfur Dioxide, or SO_2: A preservative added to wine during various stages of production, most often just before bottling to protect the wine from oxidation and unwanted bacteria. The use of sulfites in winemaking is a sore topic in natural-wine circles, with some winemakers staunchly against it and others opting to add minimal amounts to protect their wines.

Tank: A large container, often made of stainless steel, used for fermenting, ageing, and storing wine.

Tannins: Naturally occurring compounds present in grape skins, seeds, and stems that contribute to the structure of wine. Their presence in wine can also make your tongue and cheeks feel dry.

Terroir: A French term that refers to the unique combination of natural factors, including soil, climate, topography, and vineyard practices, that gives a wine its unique character.

Rares: A rare and highly sought-after wine, typically from a small or cult winery that produces limited quantities. Sometimes also referred to as "unicorns."

Vigneron: A French term for a winegrower who makes wine.

Vintage: The year in which the grapes for a particular wine were harvested.

1. In the natural wine world, lineups of empty bottles like this one at Maison Maenad signal that good times and even better wines were had.

Volatile acidity: A tasting term that refers to the presence of acetic acid and other volatile acids in wine, which can lead to nail polish and vinegar-like aromas if excessive. Sometimes also referred to as "VA."

Yeast: Microorganisms responsible for converting the sugar present in grape must into alcohol and carbon dioxide through the fermentation process. They also influence the flavor and aroma of the wine.

    Ambient, indigenous, native, wild yeast: Yeast strains naturally present on grape skins and in the winery environment.

    Commercial, inoculated, selective yeast: Yeast strains that have been selected to provide consistent fermentation results, and to allow winemakers to control the flavor profile and quality of the wine.

Zero-Zero: Natural wines produced with no added sulfites or other chemical additives, focusing on organic or biodynamic farming and minimal intervention.

How Natural Wine Is Made

Before we dive deeper into the differences between conventional and natural winemaking, let's revisit the basics of how grapes become wine.

Once grapes have reached the desired level of ripeness, they are harvested in bunches and then either kept whole or destemmed. To make white and direct-press rosé wines, the winemaker will press grapes immediately after harvest. They will then transfer the grape juice into tanks, discarding the skins, where fermentation will begin. To make red or skin-contact white wines, the winemaker will put grapes in an open tank where they will macerate with their skins and begin fermenting before being pressed. During the fermentation process, yeasts will convert sugar into alcohol, turning it into wine. Once fermentation is complete, the winemaker will transfer the wine into an ageing vessel until it is ready for bottling.

While this seems fairly straightforward, a lot can go wrong in the process. Fermentations can stall, which can give way for oxygen to be present and bacteria to thrive, turning the wine into vinegar or imparting it with faults and undesired flavor profiles. With an entire year's work at stake, winemakers only get one shot at getting it right, which is why they constantly have to be making decisions in the vineyard and in the cellar. Those decisions will vary greatly depending on whether the winemaker is working conventionally or naturally.

Wine people love to say that great wines are made in the vineyard, and there's a good reason for it. While it is true that a lot of the winemaking process happens after harvest, it is also true that healthy grapes (grapes that carry a population of wild yeast on their skins and have developed without disease or damage, resulting in optimal ripeness, balance, flavor, and appearance) will generally give a winemaker a much easier time once they reach the cellar. This is partly why we divided this section into two categories, In the Vineyard and In the Cellar, each outlining the differences between natural and conventional practices.

We also felt it was important to separate the two because it is possible for grapes to be farmed naturally and then vinified conventionally. This is sometimes the case with Organic-or Demeter-certified wines, since those certifications mostly regulate viticulture practices. We have also seen instances of conventionally grown grapes vinified in a natural way. Hopefully this distinction will help you better understand the environmental impact of the wine in your glass, as well as the ingredients that might be in it.

IN THE VINEYARD

The Conventional Vineyard

As we've discussed in What Is Natural Wine And Why Does It Matter? (p.15), conventional viticulture is tightly intertwined with the rise of industrialization and capitalism, both of which focus highly on reducing costs and labor while increasing yields to generate higher profits. Conventional vineyards are designed to tackle these objectives in a variety of ways. Unfortunately, most of them are ultimately detrimental to the environment and the production of healthy grapes. For example, selecting popular, high-yield

1. (Left) Hoses draped over a Sangiovese-filled amphora at La Ginestra in Tuscany.

vine clones and rootstocks suited to the climate is a great way to respond to consumer trends and climate challenges, but, on the flipside, doing so diminishes a vineyard's biodiversity, making it more vulnerable to pests and diseases. Machinery like tractors, harvesting machines, and pruners are invaluable tools to cut down on manual labor, but they also cause damage to the vines as well as the broader ecosystem. While irrigation systems help sustain vines in arid regions, making it possible to grow grapes in inhospitable areas, they also encourage plants to develop shallow root networks, leading to grapes of lesser quality. Systemic application of chemical fertilizers, herbicides, insecticides, and fungicides helps fight off diseases and pests while boosting yields, but ultimately it results in lifeless soil, decimated native-yeast populations, disrupted natural ecosystems, and nutrient-deficient grapes that lack depth and complexity.

The Natural Vineyard
Much like the term natural wine, natural viticulture doesn't have a single definition. Instead, it encompasses multiple farming philosophies, from the better-known organic and biodynamic farming to more obscure ones like the Fukuoka method. While the specifics vary, farming practices under the natural viticulture umbrella take a holistic approach to grape growing, recognizing their direct and long-lasting impact on the environment. This generally means that they avoid the use of chemicals; promote biodiversity in the vineyard; preserve vine diversity through *massale* selection and the reintroduction of indigenous varietals; and favor manual harvesting and pruning over the use of machinery.

In the realm of natural wine, organic farming is often considered the first phase. It involves promoting soil health and biodiversity by avoiding synthetic pesticides, herbicides, fungicides, and fertilizers. While there exists many different organic certifications across the world, such as USDA Organic (United States), EU Organic (Europe), Naturland (Germany), and EcoCert (International), several natural winemakers have chosen not to go down the certification route, citing high costs and a general lack of rigor from governing bodies.

Rooted in the teachings of controversial Austrian scientist and thinker Rudolf Steiner, biodynamic farming is often seen as organic farming's mystical cousin. Biodynamic viticulture goes a step further than simply avoiding synthetic chemicals—it incorporates spiritual and cosmic influences to make decisions that consider the entire ecosystem of the vineyard. For some grape growers, it is akin to a religion. Biodynamic practices range from incorporating animals into the vineyard to applying preparations made from plants and manure according to lunar cycles to enhance soil fertility and stimulate microbial activity. Demeter is the only organization granting biodynamic certifications around the world.

On a much smaller scale, some wine growers have taken to the teachings of Japanese farmer and philosopher Masanobu Fukuoka. His approach to farming emphasizes simplicity, minimal intervention, and creating balanced ecosystems. Unlike organic farming and biodynamic farming, Fukuoka avoids any kind of plowing or tilling in order to maintain soil structure, reduce erosion, and promote a healthy microbial environment.

IN THE CELLAR

The Conventional Winery
Conventional wineries are designed to meet industrial hygiene standards, which means they

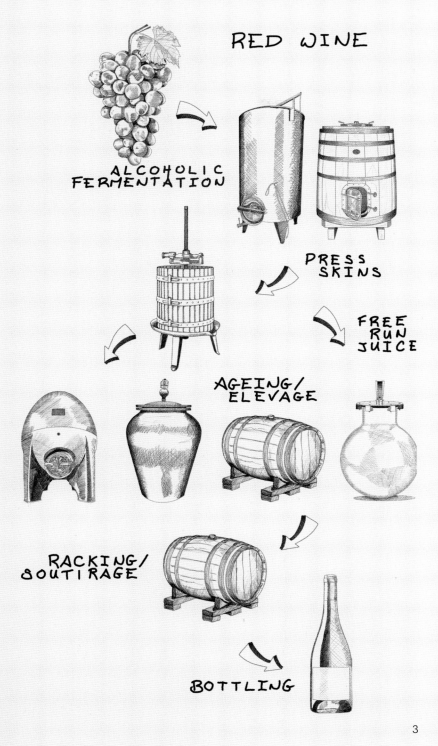

2. From conventional to natural viticulture, a fictional depiction of Xavier doing vineyard work.

3. How red wine is made: A choose-your-adventure guide to red wine

are generally equipped with sterilized stainless steel tanks, high-powered ventilation systems, and a cocktail of disinfecting products to clean equipment. The result is an environment that hinders the development of bacteria and ambient yeast. As we've established previously, the presence of yeast is needed for alcohol fermentation to occur, so when conventionally farmed grapes, their skins stripped of their indigenous yeasts, enter a sterile winery, the winemaker starts at a disadvantage. In most cases, the conventional winemaker will introduce commercial yeast to the tank alongside the grapes to initiate fermentation. That's just the beginning. We could easily fill a book of this size trying to explain every additive, machine, and process behind conventional winemaking. What is important to understand is that the tools of modern winemaking allow the winemaker to adjust virtually every aspect of a wine to make it taste, feel, and look as desired. This means that no matter how bad the raw material, how poorly the grapes were farmed, there's a powder or a machine to fix it.

Clarifying agents are used to make wine more limpid. Decolorants reduce wine saturation to make lighter rosé or red wines, while coloring agents with catchy names like Mega Purple intensify their color. Acidifiers and deacidifiers help balance off vintages. Oak tannins enrich wines, while preservatives prevent oxidation and bacterial growth post-bottling. On top of an ever-growing list of additives, larger conventional wineries are often equipped with an arsenal of high-tech tools that seem more akin to aerospace engineering than winemaking. Techniques like reverse-osmosis break down wine components to lower alcohol levels and reduce volatile acidity, while advanced filtration systems strip wine of its character, rendering it lifeless.

What are we left with once a wine has been pumped full of additives and gone through a maze of machinery? We get a wine that is completely disconnected from its origin and that can no longer even pretend to express its terroir. While it is a completely legal and common practice to do so, labeling this Frankenstein creation "wine" feels like calling grape-flavored Kool-Aid "grape juice." "Wine-based beverage" would be a more accurate description of the liquid found inside a conventional wine bottle.

The Natural Winery
It will come as no surprise that natural wineries don't share the cookie-cutter approach of conventional wineries. For this book alone we visited

wineries and cellars set inside a series of tunnels carved out of limestone, a repurposed industrial garage packed with PVC tanks, a modern brutalist structure fit for a Bond villain, and even a centuries-old château. While wildly different, they all shared common features. Usually set in naturally cool and humid environments, natural wineries do not use chemical cleaning products or high-grade ventilations systems. As a result, they foster a healthy microbiome that promotes fermentation while deterring the growth of harmful bacteria.

This means that when naturally grown grapes reach a natural winery, there is usually enough ambient yeast on the skins and in the cellar for spontaneous fermentation. Once fermentation is underway, the winemaker monitors the wine's progression to decide when to move it to an ageing vessel. As with most things related to natural wine, there is no one-size-fits-all model to what happens after that. The natural winemaker has to assess and adapt, employing a modest arsenal of tools, like temperature control, *bâtonnage*, topping up, and minimal sulfite addition (typically after malolactic fermentation and prebottling when the wine interacts with oxygen or lees).

What are we left with after the natural winemaking process is completed? Wine made with grapes and perhaps a touch of sulfites. That's it. (In contrast, conventional wines can contain dozens of ingredients, all of which remain undisclosed since there are no laws that require listing them on labels.) Ultimately, what we really get here that we don't get from a conventional wine, is a wine that encapsulates its terroir, the specific vintage—be it with higher alcohol content representative of a particularly hot summer—and the winemaker's creative decisions.

Take a Château de Béru chardonnay and compare it with one from Maison Valette. The former showcases sharp characteristics mirroring the chilly climate of Chablis, the minerality of its soil, and a more classical winemaking approach. Meanwhile, the latter boasts a golden richness and subtle oxidation, representing the warmer Mâconnais seasons and the winemaker's patient, hands-off style. Natural wine tells an unedited story, meticulously composed, while conventional wine has been rewritten to the point where the plot has been entirely lost.

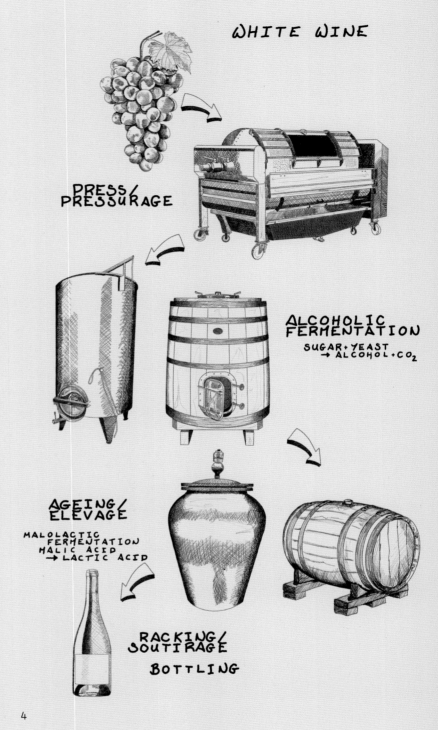

4. How white wine is made: A choose-your-adventure-with-fewer-options guide to white wine styling.

The Many Shades and Styles of Natural Wines

From orange and *pét-nats* to classical takes, natural wine contains multitudes. Here are some of the most common shades and styles you will run across.

PÉT-NAT

Short for p*étillant naturel*, *pét-nat* takes a distinctive approach to crafting sparkling wine from the more famous *méthode champenoise* (also known as the traditional method), which requires the addition of yeast and sugar to create bubbles during the secondary fermentation. To produce *pét-nat*, wine has to be bottled during fermentation, slightly before all of the sugar is done turning into alcohol. Once sealed with a crown cap, the secondary fermentation begins inside the bottle where the trapped carbon dioxide will build up and generate bubbles. Typically, the wine will remain in the bottle for several months, or even years, depending on the winemaker's preference. During this time, the sparkling wine will mature and gain character while resting on its lees (a mix of dead yeast cells and other solids left behind after the yeast has transformed the sugar into alcohol). Following this, a process called disgorging, in which the bottle is opened by hand, resulting in a lively eruption of wine and lees, removes leftover sediments. The bottle is then refilled and sealed. Achieving this kind of fermentation can be challenging and result in small amounts of residual sugar and bottle variations. Compared to traditional-method sparkling wines, *pét-nats* typically exhibit slightly deeper golden hues as well as greater richness and body because the grapes tend to be harvested when they contain enough natural sugar to complete fermentation on their own.

WHITE

While not a new style, the world of natural wine seems to have notably expanded the spectrum of white wines with hues ranging from deep gold to pale yellow. By foregoing filtration and sulfur addition, natural white wines will seldom achieve the complete clarity and transparency of wines produced by large, conventional wineries. Crafting white wine without, or with minimal, sulfur proves more challenging due to the absence of natural antioxidants typically found in red grape skins. This can result in oxidation and an increase in volatile acidity. Many of the best natural white-wine producers prioritize extended ageing, often for two to four years, which allows the wine ample time with its lees and the chance to achieve stability. That being said, with healthy grapes, thriving native yeasts, and careful cellar management, there are no reasons why great wines can't be achieved naturally.

ORANGE OR SKIN-CONTACT

Orange wine has been pivotal to the growth of the natural-wine scene. We can't possibly begin to count just how many times in our careers we've answered the question, "What is orange wine? Is it made with oranges?" It is not. It is still wine made from grapes. Typically, white wine is made by promptly crushing white grapes upon harvest, immediately separating the juice from the skins and leaving it to ferment on its own. Orange wine, on the other hand, is essentially white wine that is made like a red wine, meaning the white or gray grapes are allowed to macerate with their skins instead of being pressed directly. This process draws out color, tannins, and a myriad of flavors contained within the skins. While the roots of skin-contact wine trace back thousands of years to the country of Georgia, its modern resurgence is largely credited to a small group of visionary winemakers in the northern Italian region of Friuli, including Stanislao Stanko Radikon, Joško Gravner, and Dario Prinčič (p.176). Today, skin-contact wine is embraced worldwide, so much so that we'd be surprised if you can't find at least one bottle at your nearest wine bar.

ROSÉ

Rosé is essentially a red wine that sees shorter skin maceration to yield minimal tannin and color. Conventional rosés often imitate the pale, salmon-hued wines of Provence, characterized by their subtle pink shade. While every winemaker has their own approach, rosés within the natural-wine sphere tend to undergo slightly longer maceration, extracting a touch more color from the skins. The work of trailblazing winemaker Eric Pfifferling of Domaine de L'Anglore in Tavel, with his use of carbonic maceration, has significantly changed our perception of what rosé can be. And we can't forget the impact of Sicily legend Frank Cornelissen (p.222), whose ruby pink, highly textured Susucaru helped propel natural wine into the zeitgeist.

GLOU-GLOU RED

Glou-glou, a style of wine that is so easy to drink, you and your friends might finish a bottle faster than it would take you to spell pineau d'Aunis backward. (The French equivalent of saying "gulp-gulp," *glou-glou* evokes the sound of wine pouring rapidly in your glass or down your throat.) Often served chilled, these wines blend fruity red-wine flavors with a low-tannin, easy going vibe that can be achieved through a variety of winemaking techniques. The most popular one is carbonic maceration, a method associated with the Beaujolais, where the modern natural winemaking movement emerged. Carbonic maceration involves placing entire grape clusters, including their stems, into a sealed tank to prevent carbon dioxide from escaping during fermentation. which in turn keeps tannins soft and promotes fruitiness. Another way to achieve glou-glou red wines is to harvest grapes early to preserve acidity and keep alcohol levels low. This is often combined with a limited amount of skin contact during fermentation to control the color and extraction of the wines. Lastly, another style gaining traction is called *blouge* (a portmanteau for blanc and rouge), which involves blending red and white grape varietals, either before or after fermentation. This method allows the winemaker to use grapes with advanced phenolic maturity while preserving the wine's acidity and vibrancy.

ROBUST RED

There is a common misconception among lovers of robust red wines that natural wine is not for them. While it's true that the market at the time of the writing of this book skews toward lighter, chilled red wines, there are many incredible age-worthy big, tannic red wines being made naturally around the world. The powerful syrah wines of Northern

1

1. Amphoras, concrete tanks, and foudres in slumber at Azienda Agricola Foradori.

2. Little squirts of see-through red wine, gently extracted by pipette—a glass tool winemakers use to sample from barrels.

Rhône legend Thierry Allemand are a great example, as are the rustic teroldego wines of Italian natural-wine matriarch Elisabetta Foradori.

SWEET

Crafting sweet wine with minimal to no sulfur poses a considerable challenge. Without significant sulfur addition and filtration to remove yeasts and bacteria, wine has a tendency to want to keep fermenting until it has converted all the sugar into alcohol. While some winemakers produce brilliant, sweet cuvées, doing so typically entails achieving a sufficiently high alcohol percentage to naturally halt fermentation (around 17 to 18 percent).

2

FRANCE

REGIONS

The Loire
Burgundy
The Jura
Auvergne
The Rhône
The Languedoc

A Brief History of Natural Wine in France

France is without a doubt the country most associated with wine. While winemaking originated in the ancient Republic of Georgia around 6,000 BCE and was later adopted by the Greeks and Romans, who planted vines across Europe, it was the French who most extensively advanced viticultural and oenological practices, developed the concept of terroir, and established a framework for wine culture and education.

It comes as no surprise, then, that France would become the epicenter of the natural wine movement starting in the 1980s. Even as winemakers in other pockets of the world began to rebel against industrialized winemaking around those same years, no other place experienced such a concerted rise of the natural wine movement's ideologies as France. Why is that?

The birth of the French natural wine movement is largely attributed to the tireless collaboration among winemaker Marcel Lapierre, wine scientist Jules Chauvet, and itinerant winemaking consultant Jacques Néauport. Collaborations aside, a set of conditions specific to France certainly played a role in the movement's blossoming.

As a unified country with a central government, not only does France benefit from a shared cultural history but it also provides its citizens with a social safety net that makes them more likely to take financial risks, such as the ones involved with the production of natural wine.

The inheritance laws established in 1804 under the French civil code (known as the Napoleonic Code or the Civil Code of the French) have also had a crucial impact. Mandating that estates be divided equally among heirs, the code has encouraged a culture of small-scale, family-owned vineyards, contributing to the preservation of traditional winemaking techniques and a focus on terroir expression.

Then, of course, there's Paris. Besides being one of the most popular destinations in the world, the country's capital is also widely recognized as a cultural hub where luminaries from various fields have historically come to exchange ideas—and this was no exception for the natural wine movement.

Starting in the 1950s, Jules Chauvet began experimenting with producing wines with zero sulfites added. In the early 1980s, a young Jacques Néauport, fresh out of Beaune's viticulture college, joined Chauvet as his intern and assistant. Together, they began to produce a portion of Beaujolais winemaker Marcel Lapierre's wines without added sulfites or filtration. Marcel Lapierre quickly became a spokesperson for the movement and started producing all of his wines following Chauvet's methods.

Throughout the 1980s and 1990s, Néauport traveled around the country, spreading and applying Chauvet's ideas. In this way, Néauport effectively helped shape France's first wave of natural winemakers, collaborating with the likes of Pierre Breton and Thierry Puzelat in the Loire, Jean Foillard and Yvon Métras in the Beaujolais, Pierre Overnoy in the Jura, and Gérald Oustric in Ardèche. These winemakers have, in turn, influenced subsequent generations of natural winemakers, many of whom we feature in this book.

Inspired by the work of Marcel Lapierre and his friends, a wave of new bistros and *caves à manger* concurrently began to sprout around Paris. Starting with Les Envierges in Belleville (now closed), the list of establishments with a penchant for natural wine grew over the years to

1. A mess of bottles collects dust in the Ad Vinum cellar, the winery run by Le Châteaubriand sommelier-turned-freewheeling-winemaker Sébastien Chatillon in the Gard.

include Le Baratin, Jean-Pierre Robinot's L'Ange Vin (also closed, read more on p.38), Septime, Le Châteaubriand, and Le Verre Volé, to name a few.

In the early 2000s, the movement began to establish and organize itself. Early natural wine fairs, like La Dive Bouteille, Le Vin de Mes Amis, and 10 Vins Cochons, provided a space for winemakers to showcase their wines while exchanging ideas with other members of their flourishing community. In an attempt to define natural wine, some vignerons set out to create various certifications and organizations, including Nicolas Joly's La Renaissance des Appellations, Marcel Lapierre's L'Association des Vins Naturels, and Les Vins S.A.I.N.S, cofounded by Jean-Pierre Robinot.

Today, France accounts for roughly 25 percent of the world's surface of organic vineyards and plays host to some of the world's most influential natural-wine fairs. Across the country, bistros, bars, and restaurants keep the conversation around the movement alive year-round. Judging by Zev's frequent-flyer status, it seems that natural-wine events are happening across the country every week, proving that France remains one of the most exciting places to indulge in and to explore natural wine.

The Loire

1. Golden chenin blanc cascades out of a bottle during a cellar visit with Jean-Pierre Robinot of Domaine de L'Ange Vin.

2. After a few hours of tasting and talking in the sun, the table at Domaine Tessier tells its own story.

As a region, the Loire Valley is hard to wrap your head around—not only is it enormous and home to some of the world's most outspoken natural winemakers, but it also produces a dizzying array of wine styles from an eclectic variety of grapes.

Geographically speaking, the Loire is defined by its eponymous river—the longest in France—which rises in the Massif Central in the south, snakes its way north through the Auvergne, then shoots west through Orléans, Tours, Angers, and Nantes, before finally spilling out into the Atlantic. Underneath the region's imposing vineyard surface is a patchwork of geological formations: granite, gneiss, and schist in the west; a mix of clay, limestone, and sand in the center near Tours; finishing with the Kimmeridgian soil of Sancerre and Pouilly-Fumé in the east.

For thousands of years along the river's edges, winemakers have benefitted from the region's temperate maritime climate, influenced by the Atlantic Ocean to the west, to produce a cornucopia of grapes, ranging from the familiar gamay, pinot noir, cabernet franc, sauvignon blanc, chenin blanc, and muscadet, to the more esoteric pineau d'Aunis, romorantin, and menu pineau. The region's easygoing climate played a part in defining glou-glou, an easy-drinking style of red wine driven by fruit, lively acidity, and low alcohol levels (around 10 to 12 percent).

Glou-glou aside, the area is also capable of a stunning array of styles. Although the Loire produces a great variety of crémant (sparkling wines made using the traditional method as in Champagne), it is perhaps better known for its pétillant naturel, a style of sparkling wine made using the ancestral method (see p.25). Chenin blanc, in particular, with its refreshing acidity and savory minerality, is a magnificent candidate for *pét-nat*. The ancient volcanic hills of the Côtes d'Auvergne deliver juicy red wines with soft tannins made from pinot noir and gamay, as well as mushroomy, rich

chardonnay. Zippy, fresh wines from Sancerre and Pouilly-Fumé are known as classical expressions of sauvignon blanc. But when the grape is picked a little riper and vinified outside the appellation system, where strict rules don't apply and the wines are allowed to go through malolactic fermentation, sauvignon blanc exhibits more depth than we usually give it credit for. The mysterious, peppery and spicy pineau d'Aunis is a favorite among natural-wine lovers, and from the northern reaches of the Loire, it has become one of the most sought-after wines in production. Chinon and Bourgueil produce tannic cabernet franc wines that walk the edge between giving and bitter. And at the mouth of the Loire River lies a bed of oysters that pairs naturally well with the area's zesty and salty muscadet.

If the Beaujolais is, as it is often touted, the cradle of natural wine, then the Loire is where the movement came of age. There, in the 1990s and early aughts, a community of vociferous natural winemakers—Mark Angeli, Thierry Puzelat, and Jean-Pierre Robinot—collided to help shape the way we think about winemaking and wine drinking today. But no coming-of-age story would be complete without a great party scene, and nobody throws a wine party quite like people from the Loire. For decades running, the Loire has played host to some of the most legendary wine events, for example, La Dive Bouteille, the longest-running low-intervention wine fair, which helped define and spread the word about natural wine across the world.

In the pages that follow, you will first discover the region through the eyes of the subversive Jean-Pierre Robinot, whose contribution to the natural-wine discourse is as lengthy as his tastings. Then, we will drive about an hour and a half north to Cheverny, land of romorantin, where regional stalwart Philippe Tessier watches over his son, Simon, as he carries on the family legacy.

The recipes in this section, unlike the wines of the Loire, are simple. Prepared by the winemakers' wives Noëlla Robinot and Jocelyne Tessier, each dish speaks to the cold weather that permeated our time in the Loire. Is there a better way to face the last stretch of winter than to bite into crunchy winter crops and dig into slow-cooked, steaming hot meat dishes? We don't think so either.

WINERY   FR

Domaine de L'Ange Vin

JEAN-PIERRE & NOËLLA ROBINOT

"It's going to be a long one," says Zev as we hop in our rental car on a sunny but crisp March morning outside Saumur. "Get ready for a show," he adds, referring to our upcoming cellar visit with Jean-Pierre Robinot from Domaine de L'Ange Vin. Over the last decade, Zev has visited the famed Loire vigneron more times than he can count, which is why he has made it a habit to warn the uninitiated that they're about to experience something out of the ordinary. For Jean-Pierre Robinot is no ordinary man.

Born in the small commune of Chahaignes in Sarthe on the northern border of the Loire Valley, Jean-Pierre Robinot is among the most influential figures in France's natural-wine movement. But looking at the vigneron's eclectic resume—plumber turned wine journalist turned bistro owner turned vigneron with a passion for art and running marathons—it almost feels like a lucky accident he ended up where he is now. Jean-Pierre's life has been nothing but a series of passionate outbursts, like a meteor shower streaking through the atmosphere: bright and brilliant,

1. One of the buildings at Domaine de L'Ange Vin is adorned with a sign from Jean-Pierre Robinot's now-defunct Paris wine bar.

2. Winemaker Jean-Pierre stands with his trademark set of timeworn keys, ready to open the doors to his cellar full of liquid treasures.

3. Jean-Pierre shows us the artwork in his bathroom, a collection of cartoons which have long been a hallmark of French political commentary and natural-wine tomfoolery.

4. A mosaic of wine labels featuring Jean-Pierre's photographs, which express the movement of light and space.

unpredictable and spectacular. Anyone who catches a glimpse of Jean-Pierre Robinot feels immediately charmed.

Jean-Pierre began working as a plumber in his hometown when he was only sixteen years old in the 1960s. Soon thereafter, with only 400 francs to his name (roughly $670 today), the young man hopped on a train to Paris where he continued earning a living as a plumber while working on his art, a mix of abstract painting and photography.

In Paris, he met a group of kindred spirits, including François Morel, who would end up opening one of the city's first natural-wine bistros, Les Envierges in Belleville. Together they started diving into wine, mostly tasting bottles that we would now consider conventional wines. Then one day everything changed. "Our friend brought a bottle from Marcel Lapierre made by Jacques Néauport, at the time of Jules Chauvet in 1985," says Jean-Pierre.

"Once you're caught by the living, you can't go back," he adds, describing how energized he felt after tasting Lapierre's wine. In 1983, galvanized by the burgeoning natural-wine movement in France, he cofounded with Michel Bettane the influential wine review *Le Rouge & le Blanc* (good friend François Morel eventually joined the team as an editor). To this day, the magazine remains at the forefront of natural-wine journalism.

In 1988, after watching several of his friends open natural-wine bars across Paris, Jean-Pierre felt like his time had finally come. He scraped together the savings he amassed from twenty years working as a plumber and opened bistro L'Ange Vin (a play on the French word *angevin*, or a person from Anjou). Every night behind his zinc pulpit, he spread the natural-wine gospel to a steady clientele, who flocked to this small bistro in the 11th arrondissement as much to drink as they did for a chance to meet him.

L'Ange Vin stayed open until 2001, at which point Jean-Pierre decided to return to his native Chahaignes to try his hand at winemaking using only two of the region's indigenous grapes. Set in the broader appellation of Jasnières, an area known for producing rich and dense chenin blanc wines, the commune also overlaps with Coteaux du Loir, an appellation famous for producing pineau d'Aunis, a grape with a distinctive pepperiness that has gained cult popularity in recent years.

As soon as we arrive in Chahaignes around 10 a.m., Jean-Pierre, sporting a tiny fleece beanie flipped inside out and holding a collection of comically large keys, doesn't waste a second and immediately leads us toward his cellar. Carved out of the region's infamous tuffeau limestone (a white to light-cream, fine-grained limestone with a chalky quality) and shielded by bright green leaves and roots, the vigneron's cellar looks like something out of *The Hobbit*. It consists of a series of deep tunnels, each hidden behind thick wooden doors, in which the walls are perpetually sweating. (This hyperhumid and naturally temperature-controlled environment allows the bacteria and natural yeasts to thrive while the wines slowly bubble along during a fermentation process that can sometimes take years.)

Well into his seventies, Jean-Pierre continues to run marathons for fun at shockingly fast times. Tasting with him can very much feel like running a marathon, only one that lasts much, much longer. To start us off, Jean-Pierre searches through his giant keychain to open the first of his deep tuffeau caves. He switches on the flashlight that's affixed to his forehead and takes a few steps inside. After a few moments, he reappears, arms overflowing with bottles of *pét-nats*. With a wry smile and a wink, the vigneron pops open the first bottle, releasing an eruption of wine and lees. "May happiness flow into your glass," he says, pouring Steph the first sip. And so, the long and frenetic race to taste 100 wines begins.

With the exception of his first five vintages, in which some of the chenin blancs were kissed by a touch of sulfur to protect them as he continued traveling back and forth between his Parisian bistro and Chahaignes, Jean-Pierre makes his wines with zero additives. "If you have some basic knowledge of art history, you can identify the work of a painter right away. Wine is the same," Jean-Pierre claims. "It's the work of a man, and if he doesn't cheat, he gives a signature to the wine." Using only chenin blanc and pineau d'Aunis, Jean-Pierre produces between ten to fourteen yearly cuvées that range from dry and angular to sweet and powerful. A direct reflection of his mind, that of an artist who can't stop tinkering and creating, the wines are as distinctive as the man himself.

Over the next eight hours, Jean-Pierre guides us through a myriad of tunnels where we taste from dozens of barrels and bottles. With every pour, we gain a better appreciation for how his wines evolve throughout the fermentation process and through the years. We also sample from ten different bottles of the 2021 vintage of his sparkling pineau d'Aunis Les Années Folles to understand how bottle variation is affected by factors as simple as bottling date and storage location within the same cellar. All the while, Jean-Pierre speaks of philosophy and the cosmos, a place where his dreams seem to take him even while awake. His speech is peppered with little bits of wisdom that seem trivial at first, but that will end up staying with us. "One must always keep a secret garden inside oneself," he whispers as he opens the day's final bottle of Les Années Folles.

These tunnels are Jean-Pierre's playground. This becomes apparent not only by the excited way in which he speaks about how the cosmic energy of the caves impacts his winemaking but also by the series of surprising mold sculptures that adorn the walls. His creations, of course, Jean-Pierre's philosophy as a sculptor doesn't stray too far from his winemaking process, where he presses his grapes and lets them ferment and age with minimal intervention. For his sculptures, Jean-Pierre merely creates a framework for them to grow—in this case by bending metal wires into various shapes—and then lets nature run its course. Soon enough, mold begins to bloom around the frame, creating living sculptures that look over his living wines.

It is nearly 5 p.m. when we finally head down to the house, where Noëlla, Jean-Pierre's wife, begins to lay out a feast for us to refuel after seven hours in the cellar. As we squeeze in around the large wooden table and start smearing thick layers of rabbit terrine over crispy baguette, Jean-Pierre busies himself opening and lining up all the bottles we brought back from the caves, carefully writing the cuvée and vintage on each bottle using a white chalk pen.

Tasting through the finished wines in a controlled environment, Jean-Pierre's mastery of *élevage* and his natural showmanship are obvious. He has become a maestro of timing. The chenin blanc wines are dense and waxy, with an electrifying quality that can only be described as "Robinotesque." The pineau d'Aunis bottles range from light and almost see-through with bright peppery

5. Behind each cellar door lies a deep tunnel, home to an array of wines in various stages of *élevage*.

6. Jean-Pierre in the midst of giving us the full Robinot experience, a performance Noëlla has witnessed a million times before.

notes to dark, tannic, opulent wines where the pepper tones dip lower and deeper.

As Noëlla dishes out generous portions, Jean-Pierre waltzes around the dining room, pouring wine while talking about his abstract paintings and photographs that line the walls and shelves of their home. Some of his creations now double as wine labels, but other pieces, he says, will soon be shown to the public as part of an upcoming exhibition in Milan. In the Robinot household, the lines between art, wine, and life might be blurred, but one thing is crystal clear: in Jean-Pierre's presence, the show never ends.

ENDIVE SALAD WITH BOILED EGGS

SERVES 4

Endives are one of Noëlla Robinot's favorite winter vegetables, which is why they're usually on the menu when she cooks for friends after a lengthy tasting with Jean-Pierre. "And eggs," she says, "I always eat *a lot* of them." For this recipe, we recommend boiling your eggs for 10 minutes for a yolk that's a smidge soft, but if you prefer your yolk more firm, cook them 1 to 2 minutes longer.

INGREDIENTS

- 4 large eggs
- 4 medium endives, cut into ½-inch rounds
- 4 small shallots, peeled and thinly sliced
- 2 tbs extra-virgin olive oil
- 2 tbs apple cider vinegar
- Salt and black pepper

INSTRUCTIONS

1. Bring a small pot of water to a boil and set a medium heatproof bowl of ice water alongside. Add the eggs to the pot and cook for 10 minutes. Using a slotted spoon, remove the eggs from the pot and carefully transfer them to the ice bath. Once they're cool enough to handle, peel the eggs and cut them in half.

2. In a large salad bowl, combine the eggs, endives, and shallots. Add the olive oil, apple cider vinegar, a pinch of salt and pepper. Toss to coat. Put the salad in the fridge for 20 to 30 minutes to let the flavors marinate. Before serving, taste and adjust the seasoning with salt and pepper.

FRENCH VEAL STEW

SERVES 4-6

Blanquette de veau is like a warm hug, which is exactly what we needed after spending eight hours tasting in the cellar with Jean-Pierre. Like many traditional French recipes, its ingredients are quite humble: It can be made using regular veal shoulder cubes you find at the grocery store, or you can elevate it by asking your local butcher for a mix of braising veal cuts like neck, cheeks, shoulder, breast, a bone-in piece, or even a couple of meaty marrow bones. In the version we photographed for the book, David added a bit of smoked veal ear his butcher miraculously had on hand. Serve with a starchy side like boiled potatoes or brown rice.

INGREDIENTS

Vegetable Broth

- 2 medium carrots, peeled and cut like wine corks
- 2 leeks, rinsed and cut into 1-inch-thick rounds
- 1 medium onion, peeled and cut in half
- 2 celery stalks, cut into 1-inch-thick slices
- 4 thyme sprigs
- 2 bay leaves
- 2 tbs salt
- 1 tsp black peppercorns

Veal Stew

- 1 veal shank (about 4½ lbs), cut into 2-inch pieces
- 1 lb veal shoulder, cut into 2-inch chunks
- 6 veal cheeks, cut in half
- 6 pieces bone marrow, each about 2 inches thick (optional)
- ½ cup (1 stick) salted butter
- 3 tbs all-purpose flour
- 1 cup dry white wine, such as Jasnières
- ⅔ cup chopped carrot (2 inches)
- ⅔ cup chopped celery root (2 inches)
- ⅔ cup chopped parsnip (2 inches)
- 1 cup white button mushrooms (optional)
- 1 cup pearl onions (optional)
- 1 cup heavy cream or a dollop of salted butter (optional)
- 2 tbs chopped parsley, to finish

INSTRUCTIONS

1. **For the vegetable broth:** Place the carrots, leeks, onion, and celery in a Dutch oven or large pot. Add the thyme, bay leaves, salt, and black peppercorns, and pour in enough cold water to cover the vegetables. Bring to a simmer over medium-high heat and cook for at least 1 hour, until the broth is clear and savory. Set the broth aside until it has cooled down, then strain it through a fine-mesh sieve into an airtight container. Store the broth in the fridge until completely cold, or wait until the next day to use it.

2. **For the veal stew:** Return the cold broth to the clean Dutch oven and add the cubed veal shank, shoulder, cheeks, and marrow bones, if using. Bring to a simmer over medium-high heat, then reduce the heat to low and cook until the veal pieces are tender, about 1 hour. Remove the meat and set aside, covered, to prevent the meat from drying out. Transfer the broth to another pot and set aside.

3. Raise the heat to medium, then add the butter and flour and cook, stirring constantly to avoid lumps, until the butter has melted and combined with the flour, 2 to 3 minutes. Gradually add the broth while stirring. Add the wine, carrot, celery root, and parsnip and continue cooking until the sauce has reduced and reached a creamy consistency, about 5 minutes. Add the veal back in and cook until heated through. Depending on the season, you can add button mushrooms or pearl onions at this stage. You may also add a cup of cream or a dollop of butter and reduce until the sauce coats the back of a spoon.

4. Finish the dish with a sprinkle of parsley and serve immediately with a starchy side like boiled potatoes or brown rice.

Domaine Tessier

SIMON & PHILIPPE TESSIER

Philippe Tessier is leaning back on a chair, soaking up the high-noon sun. The winemaker's eyes are closed, their corners creased from the large smile that adorns his face. Winemakers tend to be the happy-go-lucky types, especially when they're spending time outside, but there's a certain je ne sais quoi about Philippe's relaxed demeanor on this early March afternoon.

"When my dad retired, we decided to hire him," says Simon Tessier, who took over the domaine from his father in 2020, as he ushers us in to the cellar. "He's still helping me, but in the last year and a half he's definitely slowed down a lot." Philippe's blissed-out look makes a whole lot more sense now.

Simon is the third generation of Tessier men to helm the twenty-six-hectare family estate. Located in the heart of the Cheverny and Cour-Cheverny AOCs in the Loir-et-Cher department, Domaine Tessier was established in 1961 by Simon's grandfather, Roger Tessier. After acquiring the land, Roger planted roughly five hectares of vines (a mix of gamay and romorantin), dedicating the rest of the farm to growing white asparagus and grains, as well as to raising cattle. In those early days, winemaking accounted for a rather small portion of the Tessier's operation.

Things started to change in 1981 when Roger's son Philippe took over, putting an end to the farm's asparagus, grain, and cattle activities to focus solely on grape growing and winemaking. In addition to planting more vines, Philippe thought it would be best to begin selling wine in bottles instead of selling it in bulk to the *négociants*.

Like many vignerons in the area at that time, Philippe, who had been making conventional wine the way he'd learned in school, grew increasingly interested in organic farming and natural winemaking. (The Loir-et-Cher department where Domaine Tessier is situated is home to an impressive number of natural winemakers, such as Thierry Puzelat, Hervé Villemade, and Noëlla Morantin.) Starting in 1998, Philippe converted his vineyards to organic agriculture and began to put less sulphur in his wines. Domaine Tessier now only adds sulphur at bottling unless a severe issue requires a minimal addition during fermentation.

Through his work, Philippe became an instrumental player in the preservation of the local romorantin grape varietal and the recognition of the Cour Cheverny appellation, which can only be made with romorantin. Grown almost exclusively in the Loire, romorantin is a cross between pinot teinturier, chardonnay, and gouais (a cousin of melon) that reveals floral and herbal notes supported by bright acidity.

Unlike his father, Simon Tessier did not always have winemaking aspirations. He studied sociology before eventually working in a wine

1. (Left) The garden and home adjoining the cellar at Domaine Tessier.

2. After tasting from every barrel in the cellar, lunch is in order.

shop in Nantes for six years. When Philippe started floating the idea of retiring, Simon, who had now been working in wine retail for six years, felt it was the perfect opportunity for him, his wife, Marie, and their children to move back home. Simon enrolled at the wine school in Amboise and joined his father at the domaine in preparation for the transition. Then in February 2020, Simon Tessier officially took the reins of the family estate.

"At the beginning, we were under a bit of pressure because it's a fairly important domaine in terms of volume. We were worried about getting feedback on the wines from existing customers," says Simon. "But my father never put any pressure on me at all about how I manage the day-to-day operations of the estate." While Simon has no intention to reinvent the wheel—Domaine Tessier wines are good and sell very well, after all—he has already put his twist on some elements.

Back in the cellar, one of those changes is immediately noticeable when we walk past a few shelves stacked with rolls of labels. While the names of cuvées like Les Sables, Romorantique, and Phil en Bulle are instantly recognizable, the brightly colored, geometric labels are unfamiliar. The work of Marie, who left her career as a graphic designer to join her husband at the domaine, the new labels denote a new era for this old-school natural-wine estate. But in a world of natural-wine labels dominated by cartoons, Marie's minimalist designs err on the classical side of the spectrum.

As for the winemaking, Simon hasn't made changes to existing cuvées but is working on new wines, experimenting with different ageing vessels such as sandstone amphoras (Philippe was already using Georgian-style clay amphoras for certain cuvées). In the vines, Simon hopes to further push what his father had started and convert the vineyards to biodynamic agriculture. "With Marie and my dad, we would like to start experimenting a bit," says the young winemaker. "Maybe start by making some herbal teas and preparations for a couple parcels, then see how the plants respond."

Family successions are a common trope in television and movies because they are often ripe with conflict. Can a child ever live up to the legacy of their parents or will their mistakes tarnish it? Should a successor be allowed to implement change, and can they do so without denaturing the family business? While it is true that transitions can be sticky, especially when egos are involved, the Tessier family proves there is a gentler path to succession, one that is colored with trust.

When we come out of the cellar, Philippe is waiting for us with a bottle of Phil en Bulle (a sparkling blend of romorantin and orbois). Elated with our tasting with Simon, we gush to Philippe about our favorite cuvées and the new labels. With a knowing look in his eyes, Philippe proudly raises his glass: "Santé!"

3

3. Winemaker Simon Tessier contemplating the cellar that he recently inherited from his father.

4. Jocelyne Tessier (foreground) and her husband Philippe Tessier, who despite no longer running the domaine still enjoys showing up for tastings and leisurely lunches.

BEER-BRAISED RABBIT WITH PRUNES

SERVES 2–4

Known in French as lapin aux pruneaux, this classic dish is most often associated with the farmhouse cooking traditions of southern France, where prunes and wine abound. This variation, which incorporates beer in the braising liquid instead of wine, can be found in various northern regions such as Brittany, where Jocelyne Tessier grew up. "My grandparents were farmers in the countryside, where prunes are often associated with braised meat dishes," she says. "In the winter, when there was no fresh fruit around, we would buy prunes made with dried plums from southwestern France." For this recipe, look for Agen prunes, a protected and relatively plump variety grown in the Lot-et-Garonne department. As for the rabbit, if you're up for it, you can buy it whole and cut it yourself, but we suggest saving yourself the trouble and asking your butcher to do that for you.

INGREDIENTS

- 1 whole rabbit (about 3 lbs), cut into 6 to 8 pieces
- 1 **tbs** salt
- 1 **tsp** black pepper
- 4 **tbs** extra-virgin olive oil
- ¼ **cup** cognac
- 1 medium onion, finely chopped
- 4 garlic cloves, minced
- 2 medium carrots, peeled and finely chopped
- 1 **tbs** honey
- 2 **tbs** fresh herbs (we like a mix of thyme, tarragon, oregano, and marjoram)
- 2 (12-oz) bottles (1½ cups) amber beer
- 6 pitted prunes, preferably from Agen prunes

INSTRUCTIONS

1. Pat the rabbit pieces dry and season with salt and pepper. Heat 2 tbs of the olive oil in a large Dutch oven set over medium-high heat. Add the rabbit pieces and sear until golden, 3 minutes on each side. Remove from the heat and carefully pour out the fat. Add in the cognac and then use a long barbecue lighter to light it up. (This is a technique called flambé, which imparts the meat with a lot of flavor from the cognac while cooking off the alcohol.) Once the flames have gone out on their own, remove the meat and set aside.

2. Set the Dutch oven over medium heat, then add the remaining 2 tbs olive oil, the onions, garlic, carrots, and honey and sweat until the vegetables have started to soften, 3 to 5 minutes. Return the rabbit pieces to the Dutch oven and add the herbs. Pour in the beer and bring to a boil. Reduce the heat to low, cover the pot, and simmer for 45 minutes, until the rabbit is tender. Stir in the prunes and continue cooking for another 15 minutes, until the broth has reduced, leaving the rabbit only half covered. Serve immediately.

The Jura

1. (Left) Tucked in the heart of Arbois, Le Bistrot des Claquets is the quintessential natural-wine spot and gossip hub for the Jura wine community.

It's hard to believe that the Jura was once one of the most obscure wine regions in France. Until fairly recently, most wine books only made a quick mention of it as the birthplace of vin jaune and vin de paille, completely disregarding the wide variety of wines produced in the area. Nowadays, it's a whole different story. Jura's wild wines are on everyone's lips, with prized bottles from producers like Pierre Overnoy and Kenjiro Kagami commanding astronomical prices at wine auctions. How did such a dramatic shift happen so quickly?

Tucked in the foothills of the Alps, the Jura is a miniscule winegrowing region—just under 2,000 hectares—that conjures every possible mental imagery you may have of rural France. Cold streams flow down the mountains, passing through old mills to collect in quaint village centers. Vast forests carpeted by mushrooms and moss engulf steep vineyards. Cows graze on lush farmlands to produce milk for the region's famed Comté, Vacherin Mont d'Or, and Morbier cheeses.

Standing on a mix of marl, limestone, clay, and schist, the Jura is best known for vin de paille (a golden sweet wine made by drying out handpicked grapes on straw beds) and vin jaune (a wine unique to the Jura made exclusively from savagnin grapes) and the traditional winemaking style sous-voile (under veil). Instead of topping up barrels to avoid oxidation as the wine ages and slowly evaporates, Jura winemakers allow the local yeast strains to form a layer of mold called voile, which protects the wine from oxidation and imprints it with a distinctive nutty and saline tang that can't be replicated anywhere else.

While inimitable, these traditional Jurassien wines did little to bring Jura out of relative obscurity. Rather it was the work of a forward-thinking community of natural winemakers, starting with Pupillin luminary Pierre Overnoy, who in 1984 began to practice topped-up Burgundian-style ageing on his white wines. Sought after by classical sommeliers and natural-wine nerds alike, Overnoy's wines have become some of the most difficult to acquire. Other legendary winemakers, like Jean-François Ganevat, whose imposing presence looms large in the southern Jura, followed suit and began producing mineral-forward and angular wines that contrast with the traditional Jurassien styles.

The new wave of Jura wines showcases the region's five indigenous grape varietals. The thin-skinned poulsard creates light, bright, and fun red wines with an elusive see-through quality that's been emulated the world over. Trousseau makes for denser and darker wines that carry distinctively Jurassien earthy tones, while pinot noir takes on an elevated liveliness when grown in the Jura, where the northeastern bise wind blows, reducing humidity levels and slowing down the ripening process of the grapes to preserve freshness.

Made from the aforementioned savagnin as well as chardonnay, the white wines of the Jura are characterized by their incisiveness and sharp cheese-like savoriness imparted by the region's native yeasts. Several producers, like Ganevat and neighbor Julien Labet, prefer releasing single-parcel wines, especially for the whites, whose salty qualities, reminiscent of minerality, tend to better reflect the elusive nuances of their terroir.

In the next pages, you will become acquainted with expat winemakers from Maison Maenad and Domaine des Miroirs, who exemplify two sides of the Jura wine boom: the electrifying excitement of establishing a new domaine and the uncomfortable dilemma that comes with selling small-batched wine from such a hyped region. Each recipe in this chapter, prepared for us with local meats and vegetables, acts as a love letter to the small-scale agricultural traditions of the winemakers' adoptive country.

Maison Maenad

KATIE WOROBECK

Steph instantly perks up like a dog hearing its owner's voice the moment we arrive at the bottom of one of Maison Maenad's parcels of ripe savagnin. "My people!" she exclaims, recognizing the familiar Quebecois accents echoing throughout the south Jura's deep valleys. Not only is most of the harvest crew from Montreal, but some of them have even guided the authors of this book through countless meals and bottles at some of the city's best restaurants.

"I wanted to work harvest this year but I wasn't sure where to go," answers Florence Fortin-Houle, a manager at Joe Beef's sister restaurant Vin Papillon, when Steph asks how she ended up here. "Everyone told us to reach out to Katie."

Picking grapes a few rows over, with her dark brown hair wrapped in a messy bun, Katie Worobeck is somewhat of a Canadian success story in natural-wine circles. A force to be reckoned with, the Ottawa native is incredibly smart, resolute, and exceptionally welcoming. It's easy to understand why Katie comes highly recommended.

Like many of her peers in this book, Katie's path to winemaking wasn't straightforward. She started out with dreams of working in academia with a focus on small-scale agriculture. But after meeting a farmer at the Ottawa restaurant where she curated the wine program and he invited her to visit his farm, her perspective shifted. "I started farming and spending all my days off there. I really wanted to learn about organic farming by actually doing it, not just studying it," she explains.

1

2

Katie abandoned her studies and started working at a winery in southern Ontario, where she quickly became the assistant winemaker. The job was hard and the hours long but it confirmed she had the stamina necessary to one day run her own project. Every Sunday, the winery team hosted large communal dinners. Restaurant folks from Montreal and Toronto would drive up with cases upon cases of the latest natural-wine arrivals. "That's where I learned about tasting wine," says Katie.

Eager to learn more about natural winemaking, she asked her friend and the coauthor of this book, David McMillan, to contact his pal, the legendary Jura winemaker Jean-François Ganevat, about a stage. Widely regarded as one of the world's leading natural winemakers, Ganevat produces a wide range of sought-after wines, including whites made from chardonnay and savagnin, reds from pinot noir, poulsard, and trousseau, sparkling wines, as well as vin jaune, a style of oxidative savagnin unique to the region. Ganevat (or Fanfan, as his friends call him) invited Katie to the hamlet of La Combe de Rotalier in the southern Jura to stay with him and his wife, Anne, for the 2016 harvest, bottling, and pruning seasons.

During those six months, Katie received a crash course in natural winemaking from a master, whose attention to detail is unparalleled. "Tasting through wines that had been there for years was very formative," she says. "I'm not a supertaster, but it gave me a lot of confidence in knowing the kinds of wines I like and knowing that I can make wines like that."

Beyond imparting numerous lessons in winemaking, the Ganevat family inadvertently offered the young Canadian winemaker a master class in hospitality. "The tastings at Ganevat are really long, not only because there's so much wine to taste through but because everyone eats together at the end," says Katie. "When people come to the domaine, it's like 'come in, have a drink, have a coffee with us.' There's always a moment to just have fun and share. It's real hospitality on a human level."

In the blink of an eye, six months turned into two years, during which Katie became Ganevat's assistant winemaker and grew the confidence to start thinking about her own winemaking project. Then one day, during the 2018 harvest, a retiring grape grower walked in the Ganevat cellar as Katie and Fanfan were cleaning the press. He was looking to part ways with eight hectares of vines and invited the duo to visit one

1. After all the juice has been squeezed out of the grapes, the leftovers get foot-stomped in tanks before heading to the cellar.

2. Steph daydreams in Maison Maenad's vineyard, exhausted after picking half a bin of grapes.

of his high-altitude parcels in Saint-Laurent-la-Roche (now La Chailleuse). It was located across the valley from Ganevat's famed En Billat plot, where Katie spent countless hours working.

"It's so beautiful out there, and I remember staring across the valley, at the vines with a little cabin in the middle, thinking that I'd like to have something like that for myself one day," recounts Katie. "Then when we arrived, those were the exact vines I would look at all the time and I was like, no way, this has to be mine.'"

Katie convinced the man to sell her five hectares for her to start her own project, Maison Maenad, which she named after the wild women depicted in the stories of Dionysus, the god of wine and pleasure. "The name feels subtly feminist," states Katie. Famous for their ecstatic celebrations, which often involved dancing and drinking, the Maenads were also known for challenging traditional gender roles and expectations through their rejection of conventional social norms. (They lived in the woods, were unmarried, and loved having a good time.)

Katie continued to work with Ganevat through 2020 while producing Maison Maenad's first vintage using gamay, chardonnay, and a field blend of hybrid grape varietals. While reds made from hybrids have a reputation for tasting foxy (musty), Katie's came out fresh and hyper-fruity. An overnight success within the natural-wine scene, Maison Maenad's wines can now be found on some of the best lists back home in Canada and in the United States. Despite the early recognition, Katie seems comfortable in her position, likely due to her experience alongside Ganevat and her ability to surround herself with friends who champion her vision.

Always one to plan ahead, the winemaker often thinks about the future of Maison Maenad. In the short term, she wants to expand with more cuvées and push her sustainable agricultural practices further. "I'm really excited to make it as dynamic as possible," she says. "I want to get animals in the vines and I want to start planting things that aren't vines. This is the project of a lifetime." When asked about Maison Maenad's

3. Katie Worobeck gets ready to pull some chickens out of the oven.

4. Zev loads the press at Maison Maenad.

future beyond her own, Katie's hospitable nature, and inclination to involve others, shines through.

"I've been trying to think about whether this could be a collaborative project. I don't have kids that are going to take over, but I know how hard it is to be a woman in agriculture. It could be a shared place where women can come and have a learning experience," she reflects.

In choosing the name Maison Maenad for her winery, Katie may have inadvertently foretold its future as a haven where other wild women like herself can flourish.

4

ROAST CHICKEN WITH MORELS AND VIN JAUNE

SERVES 6–8

This recipe is Katie's love letter to high-quality chicken. "I never really loved chicken until I started eating it in France," she says. "I've never seen chicken like that outside of France, and the first time I ate it, it was like eating chicken for the first time." This being one of the most quintessential dishes from the Jura, there exist many versions and ways to prepare it. None are wrong. But there are some key factors to keep in mind to make it as rich and special as possible. The chicken must be of the highest quality (it doesn't need to be French, but it must be organic), the morels should be plump and generous, and, most importantly, the sauce should taste of pure vin jaune. In this version, we roast the chicken first and assemble the sauce using scrapings from the pan, and the hat trick is to add vin jaune to the sauce at the very end for that extra *Jurassien* taste.

INGREDIENTS

- 2 whole chickens (approximately 3½ lbs each), legs trussed
- salt
- black pepper
- 1 **tbs** extra-virgin olive oil
- 4 medium shallots, chopped
- 2 garlic cloves
- 2 sprigs of thyme
- 1 **tbs** Dijon mustard
- ¼ **cup** + 2 **tbs** vin jaune
- 1 **cup** fresh morels, cleaned, or 2 oz dried morels, soaked in water
- 2 **cups** heavy cream
- ¼ **cup** salted butter

INSTRUCTIONS

1. Preheat the oven to 375°F.

2. Generously season the chickens inside and out with the salt and pepper. Coat a large roasting tray with the olive oil and place the seasoned chickens inside. Transfer to the oven and roast, basting every 20 minutes, for 1½ to 2 hours, or until the chickens achieve a golden brown color. Lower the oven temperature to 300°F.

3. Transfer the chickens from the roasting tray to a cutting board. Skim off and discard approximately 80 percent of the fat from the tray. Pour the remaining fat into a medium pot set over medium heat, and use a wooden spoon to scrape in any flavorful bits from the roasting tray. Add the shallots, garlic, thyme, mustard, and 2 tbs vin jaune to the medium pot, and stir to remove any bits that have stuck to the bottom of the pot. Add the morels, cream, and butter and bring the mixture to simmer.

4. Untie the chickens and cut each one into 6 pieces. Arrange the chicken pieces, skin side up, in 1 large or 2 smaller ovenproof dishes. Add the remaining ¼ cup vin jaune to the simmering and thickened cream and morel sauce. (This step is the key to enhancing the flavor of the dish.) Pour the cream and morel sauce over the chicken pieces.

5. Return the chickens to the oven for 20 to 30 minutes, until the sauce is bubbling. Serve with Salad with Pea Vinaigrette (p. 62) and a side of fresh country bread.

SALAD WITH PEA VINAIGRETTE

SERVES 4-6

This salad is near perfect for a hot summer day. Serve it in lieu of potatoes as a side for roast chicken, fish, beef, or lamb. You could even add a little honey drizzle if you feel sweet, or a little lemon juice if you feel tart.

INGREDIENTS

- 3 heads little gem or butter lettuces, chilled, split in four or leaves pulled
- 1 **tbs** Dijon mustard
- 1 **tbs** sherry vinegar
- 1 **tbs** finely chopped chervil leaves
- 1 **tbs** finely chopped tarragon leaves
- ¼ **cup** heavy cream
- 2 **tbs** extra-virgin olive oil
- Salt and black pepper
- 1 **cup** frozen green peas, thawed (or fresh peas, blanched and chilled)

INSTRUCTIONS

1. Dress a large plate with the lettuce, making sure to create beautiful cups with the leaves.

2. In a medium bowl, combine the mustard, vinegar, chervil, tarragon, cream, olive oil, and pinch of salt and pepper. Add the peas to the vinaigrette and stir to combine. Taste and adjust the seasoning with salt and pepper. Pour the vinaigrette over the lettuce and serve immediately.

Domaine des Miroirs

KENJIRO & MAYUMI KAGAMI

A dumbfounded look washes over Zev's face. "They need help with harvest and said we can come lend a hand tomorrow!" he announces, moments after hanging up the phone with Kenjiro and Mayumi Kagami, the elusive couple behind the cult Jura winery Domaine des Miroirs. Zev is beaming.

Easily recognizable by their labels featuring cloudy blue skies, Domaine des Miroirs wines are sometimes referred to as unicorn wines or, more plainly among our wine friends, as "rares." Wines that fall under that umbrella are in high demand, extremely hard to find, and typically command astronomical prices on the market. (At the time of writing, a single bottle of Domaine des Miroirs can be purchased online for anywhere between $1,000 and $6,000.) Additionally, the lore behind a rare wine's winemaker plays a significant role in its appeal and notoriety. This case is no exception—even long before Kenjiro started Domaine des Miroirs, his story was the stuff of legends.

Born in Japan, Kenjiro worked as an engineer for Hitachi before becoming a winemaker. In the late 1990s, inspired by his mother's fervent love of European culture, the young man left his homeland to study oenology in Beaune. During that time, he learned the ropes working at the legendary Domaine Comte Georges de Vogüé in Burgundy's Chambolle-Musigny. Near the end of his studies in 2004, with his ambition turning toward natural winemaking, Kenjiro landed a job working for Thierry Allemand in the steep hills of Cornas. Before the year was over, he was summoned by another natural-wine legend, the Alsatian winemaker Bruno Schueller. Kenjiro worked as Schueller's cellar master until 2011. That year, encouraged by his friend and mentor, the mythic Jura winemaker Jean-François Ganevat, Kenjiro planted roots in the hamlet of Grusses and started Domaine des Miroirs.

The meaning behind the domaine's esoteric name is twofold, according to Kenjiro and Mayumi. At its most literal level, it is a direct translation of the winemaker's last name—Kagami is Japanese for "mirrors" (*miroirs* in French). "The other reason," explains Kenjiro, "is that we wanted our philosophy and our way of life to be reflected in the wines we made."

As for the iconic label, it comes from a picture Kenjiro took of the sky above their vineyard, which he modified to look more like a painting. The couple believes that the clouds are also reminiscent of those seen through an airplane window. Playing on that idea, the name of their first cuvée, "Où est-ce qu'on part? On verra bien" (Where are we going? We shall see) underscored the beginning of their journey as winemakers, as well as their noninterventionist ethos.

The following day, dizzy with excitement, we finally reach the bottom of the domaine's steep slopes. Surrounded by forest, the crescent-shaped five-hectare vineyard seems to envelop us in a sunny embrace. Above us, a few white clouds float over an otherwise blue sky, prompting us to hum "This Must Be the Place" by the Talking Heads as Mayumi leads us to the top of a row of poulsard, where we are to begin picking grapes.

Kenjiro's passion for biodynamic and no-till farming is quickly apparent when we see the vines up close: heavy with grapes, they are dense with tall grasses and other wild vegetation. (A challenging practice that avoids disturbing the soil through tillage, no-till agriculture, when done

1. (Left) Mayumi Kagami rinses vegetables in her kitchen sink after a long morning of harvest.

2. Mayumi and Zev walk bins full of savagnin grapes down a steep hill.

properly, helps maintain soil health and structure and improves water retention.) While yields vary from year to year, they tend to be remarkably low here compared to the rest of the region, typically hovering between twenty and thirty hectoliters per hectare. In recent years, climate change has also made it even more challenging for the couple, with some of their vintages, such as 2017 and 2022, getting almost completely wiped out by frost.

Before we begin, Mayumi goes over their meticulous method of triage, which happens during picking rather than in the cellar, as is sometimes the case in other domaines. Each bunch is to be thoroughly inspected, and each grape that exhibits potential faults (discoloration, bug bites, or dryness) is to be discarded to ensure only healthy grapes make it to the cellar. When it comes to making natural wine, especially without sulfur, as is the case here, the devil is in the details—and the Kagamis are nothing if not detail-oriented. "If you are not sure, taste grapes until you know the difference between a good and a bad grape," instructs Mayumi.

We make our way through the first row at a glacial pace, tasting enough thin-skinned poulsard grapes to rival a Brooklyn restaurant's yearly allocation. Slowly, we begin to understand why Domaine des Miroirs is known for its limited quantities—a fact that contributes to the staggering prices their wines command on the market.

An easy way to understand how some of these wines reach such exorbitant prices is to compare restaurants, wine shops, and auctions to ticket-resale platforms, where high-demand concert tickets routinely sell for drastically higher prices than what was originally set by the artist. When it centers around inflated ticket prices for a pop star's multibillion-dollar world tour, the conversation around the unjust reality of resale platforms might make headlines, but it won't make us feel too bad. But when the same principles apply to the work of small-scale farmers practicing biodynamic agriculture in the French countryside, this capitalism-coated pill is a lot harder to swallow.

While there are general industry standards for wine markups (three to four times is the going rate in New York restaurants), there is no legislation around what businesses are allowed to charge for a certain product. To put this in perspective, allow us to use real numbers we've encountered for Domaine des Miroirs wines (but keep in mind that prices are subject to change depending on factors like yearly yields and demand).

3

Let's say Kenjiro decides to price a bottle of wine at around $50 to cover his production costs, frost damage, and living expenses. He sells it to an importer like Zev, who, in turn, sells it to a retailer or restaurant for about $90. Now, this is where things get a little sticky. By the time that same bottle lands on a restaurant's wine list or in a retail store, it will be priced around $1,200 (prices at auction will certainly creep even higher than that). This means that the final reseller will turn a generous profit, while Kenjiro won't see a dollar above the initial $50.

Around 1 p.m, Kenjiro and Mayumi invite us back to their house, a small farmhouse that doubles as their winery and cellar. Consisting of only a few rooms, the Kagami residence is cozy. A dozen empty bottles of Domaine des Miroirs line the shelves above the stove. In the dining

3. Emmanuel Kovarik from Les Jardins de Grusse, a biodynamic farm down the road from Domaine des Miroirs.

4. Winemaker Kenjiro Kagami.

5. A table inside the greenhouse at Les Jardins de Grusse.

room, piles of books crowd the space, giving it a warm, lived-in character.

As we set the table for lunch, Kenjiro grabs an unmarked bottle and, using a blue chalk pen, scribbles "Berceau '15." Only produced in 2011 and 2015, Berceau is exemplary of Domaine des Miroirs wines. Made up of 100 percent chardonnay, the wine is focused and angular, while also shining with fruit and complexity. The large majority of the domaine's production consists of white wines made with chardonnay as well as the local savagnin. Each parcel is harvested, fermented, and bottled separately to showcase its distinct character. The savagnin cuvées are generally razor sharp, fitting the textbook definition for minerality in wine. The few bottles of red wine produced vary year to year, ranging from feather light to bordering on medium bodied.

As we dig into Mayumi's nourishing Nikujaga (see recipe on p. 72), Kenjiro mentions they're currently saving up to build an extension to their cellar. Part of what makes Domaine des Miroirs wines so incredible is that Kenjiro is extremely sensitive to *élevage*, preferring to release wines when he deems them ready rather than chronologically. Since some wines are aged for five to eight years before release, the expansion would allow the winemaker for more storage space, among other things.

When asked why he doesn't simply raise his prices, given that his wines end up being sold for thousands of dollars regardless, Kenjiro stays humble. "If we keep going that way, our wines will only be for rich people. It's important for us to remain accessible," he says. To illustrate the strength of his conviction, the winemaker tells the story of how he once ended a long-term direct partnership with a wine store after he found out they were overcharging customers for his wines.

Despite some arguing that it's foolish for the winemaker not to raise his prices, allowing other players on the wine market to profit from his work, Kenjiro remains in control of what's always mattered most to him and Mayumi: making wine that reflects their values. "Paying $4,000 for a bottle?" exclaims Kenjiro, laughing. "It's not a car. It's not jewelry. It's just wine. You drink it and it's over." Perhaps it's time we all take a look in the mirror and ask ourselves, who's really the fool now?

6. The piano in the Kagami family's living room, currently used to display items.

7. (Right) Cloudy with a chance of rares.

WINERY FR

CARROT SALAD WITH LENTILS, SHISO, AND SESAME SEEDS

SERVES 4–6

Grated carrot salads are popular side dishes in both France and Japan, the Kagami family's native country. In Japan, various grated carrot salads exist, ranging from fresh, stir-fried, and steamed versions dressed with soy sauce and sesame seeds to subtly pickled side salads. In France, carottes râpées typically features grated or julienned carrots seasoned with olive oil, lemon juice, and Dijon mustard, garnished with fresh parsley. Mayumi's version, in which torn shiso plays the part of parsley, incorporates a red wine vinegar and olive oil dressing, complemented by sesame seeds, striking a delightful balance between a French and a Japanese carrot salad.

INGREDIENTS

Salt
1 cup black or brown lentils, rinsed
4 cups grated carrots
3 tbs red wine vinegar, plus more as needed
3 tbs extra-virgin olive oil
Flaky sea salt, to taste
2 tbs toasted sesame seeds
6 shiso leaves, roughly torn

INSTRUCTIONS

1. In a medium pot of salted water, add the lentils and bring to a boil. Cover, then reduce the heat to low and simmer until the lentils are tender but not mushy. (The amount of time will depend on the size of your lentils.) Drain and set aside to cool.

2. In a large bowl, combine the carrots and lentils. Add the vinegar and olive oil. Toss to combine. Taste and adjust the seasoning with vinegar and flaky sea salt. Add the sesame seeds and shiso leaves. Toss again and serve immediately.

NIKUJAGA WITH YUZU KOSHO

SERVES 4–6

Now a beloved comfort food around Japan, Nikujaga is a fairly recent addition to the country's culinary repertoire. It first appeared in the late nineteenth century when western influences were introduced to Japan under Emperor Meiji who, among many other things, lifted the country's ban on red meat. While Nikujaga draws inspiration from Western beef and potato stews, its broth, made with soy sauce, mirin, sake, and dashi (Japanese soup stock) is fundamentally Japanese. Mayumi's version was prepared for us during harvest a day ahead of time (to allow the flavors to develop) using freshly picked vegetables grown by her friend, the biodynamic farmer Emmanuel Kovarik at Les Jardins de Grusse, down the road from the winery. For an extra kick, enjoy this with a dollop of yuzu kosho (a fermented Japanese condiment made from fresh chilies, salt, and yuzu citrus zest and juice).

INGREDIENTS

- 2¾ **lbs** beef chuck (or other boneless stewing beef), cut into 2-inch cubes
- 1¼ **cups** sake
- 1 square dried kombu
- 1 small piece of ginger
- ½ small leek, rinsed
- 12 medium yellow potatoes, cut into bite-sized pieces
- 6 medium carrots, cut into bite-sized pieces
- 6 medium onions, cut into bite-sized pieces
- ½ **cup** mirin
- ¾ **cup** soy sauce
- Salt
- Yuzo kosho, for serving (optional)

INSTRUCTIONS

1. In a large pot, combine the beef, sake, kombu, ginger, and leek. Add cold water to cover. Bring to a simmer over medium heat and cook until the beef is tender, at least 1 hour. Remove the beef, kombu, ginger, and leek from the pot. Set the beef aside, discarding the kombu, ginger, and leek.

2. Add the potatoes, carrots, and onions to the remaining liquid along with the mirin and soy sauce. Simmer for about 30 minutes. Return the cooked beef to the pot and continue simmering until the vegetables are soft but not mushy, an additional 30 minutes. Taste and adjust the seasoning with salt. Serve immediately with a dollop of yuzu kosho, if desired.

Burgundy

Burgundy is perhaps the most well-known and respected wine region in the world, partly thanks to its long winemaking history and revered appellation system. But fame has come with a price: as the birthplace of some of the world's most expensive and sought-after wines, Burgundy proves that the more famous a wine region is the more challenging it is for it to evolve.

Standing on mostly chardonnay and pinot noir, with some aligoté, pinot gris, and misfit varieties like césar, Burgundy produces a stunning array of wines. In the north, the Yonne department represents the higher acidity, angular wines stemming from Chablis's characteristic Kimmeridgian marl soils, and lesser-known appellations like Vézelay, Irancy, and Auxerre. Drive an hour and a half south to the Côte d'Or, and you will brush shoulders with devout wine fans looking for a taste of what are believed to be the highest expressions of pinot noir and chardonnay, from hallowed appellations like Puligny-Montrachet, Meursault, and Gevrey-Chambertin. If you continue south on the A6 for about an hour, you will make your way through the Côtes Chalonnaise, where red and white appellations like Mercurey and Rully fly under the radar. Keep going and you will find yourself on the border of the Beaujolais, in one of the country's most underrated wine regions, the Mâconnais, where the only ruler, chardonnay, reaches new depths.

With wines that range from the super accessible to the you-can't-get-this kind of bottles, as well as plenty of hidden treasures that will remind you why you fell in love with the region in the first place, Burgundy is a true wine nerd's paradise. So, if it ain't broke, don't fix it, right? Well, that all depends on your definition of "broke." From our vantage point, the cracks in the Burgundian system run deep.

The region's entire appellation system, which largely influences the astronomical prices of certain bottles, is based on the concept of terroir. (Terroir encompasses factors like soil, climate, topography, and traditional winemaking practices). Burgundy harbors hundreds of appellations and *lieux-dits* (historical, geographical places) that are divided into four classes: Regional, Village, Premier Cru, and Grand Cru. As you move up the hierarchy, the wines generally get more expensive and are expected to showcase increasing levels of complexity, while also expressing the unique characteristics of individual villages, vineyards, or parcels—even when those locations are as close as twenty feet from one another. (In contrast, the appellation system in Bordeaux primarily focuses on the reputation of the châteaux or producers.)

Basically, the appellation system in Burgundy aims to create a link between the geographical origin of a wine and its sensory attributes, while also helping ensure a certain level of quality and consistency within an appellation. At least that was its intention when it was first put in place in 1935, a few decades before industrial winemaking techniques took the wine world by storm, prioritizing consistency and mass production over the distinctiveness of terroir.

As we've discussed earlier in this book (p.16), when additives and interventions are employed excessively to correct flaws or modify the organoleptic (or sense) characteristics of a wine, it can undermine the true expression of terroir. In the case of Burgundy, working in this way completely dilutes the significance of an appellation system and pricing model that is based on terroir.

If the variances of soil and location have such a significant impact on a wine, as the appellations would have us believe, shouldn't the parcel's native yeasts be protected as well? And if we are to believe—and many do—that pinot noir is a direct reflection of a vintage and its weather, wouldn't chaptalization (the process of adding sugar to a wine, often to balance an unripe vintage), a very common practice in Burgundy, alter the true story of that wine?

Natural winemaking, on the other hand, with its minimal intervention approach, allows the grapes and terroir to speak for themselves and prioritize a more authentic expression of the wine's origin. But the reality is that, given the prices the region's wines command, very few Burgundian estates are willing to take the risk of making the transition to natural viticulture and winemaking. While farming without systemic chemical pesticides, herbicides, and fertilizers might lead to healthier soil, vines, and grapes, it can often result in lower grape yields, increased labor costs and profit loss.

In this section, you will meet a group of winemakers who represent the past and future of a better, truer Burgundy. From Chablis to the Mâconnais, these domaines, which include Château de Béru, Les Faverelles, Marthe Henry, Chandon de Briailles, Maison en Belles Lies, and Maison Valette, have been on a quest to improve farming practices and make wines with fewer additives to honor their region's sacred terroirs.

Our visit to Burgundy coincided with harvest season, a special time of year where people from all over the world converge to work long days, eat gargantuan communal meals, and talk for hours. The recipes that follow, a mix of traditional Burgundian dishes and tried-and-true family recipes, aim to reflect the ebullient spirit of harvest. Most are hearty, protein-heavy, and can easily be doubled or tripled—ideal when you have to feed an army of hard-working grape pickers.

Château de Béru

ATHÉNAÏS DE BÉRU

It's hard to get lost on your way to meet Athénaïs de Béru. Whether you're driving from Paris or Beaune, you get off the A6 and follow signs to Chablis until her last name becomes ubiquitous. If you're approaching from the south, as we are on this mid-September afternoon, you will find yourself at the bottom of a deep valley. There, a series of signs reading Béru and Château de Béru will urge you to take a sharp left onto a road that switchbacks up the hill on which presides the aforementioned Château de Béru, where the iconoclast winemaker is expecting us. Calling Athénaïs an outsider can seem like a bit of a stretch, given that the village in which we find ourselves bears her name. But in so many ways, that's what she is.

Athénaïs did not grow up in Chablis with the intention of becoming a winemaker. Shortly after she was born, her family relocated to Paris and leased their estate's fourteen hectares of vines to a grape farmer who sold the fruit to a local cooperative. While they spent most weekends and vacations at the château, Athénaïs very much grew up in the city, where she studied and worked in finance, specializing in mergers and acquisitions. In 2004, as the farmer responsible for the estate was set to retire, the Béru family was faced with a choice: find a new leasee or farm the land themselves, something none of them had ever done before. "When I was little, my parents would send me to the cellar with a flashlight and say 'tonight we're making a pot-au-feu, pick a wine to go with it,'" recounts Athénaïs. "Wine was always a big part of our lives, but I didn't know anything about the technical side of it. I saw this as an opportunity to pick things up where my family left off."

The first four years were intense to say the least. Athénaïs kept working in Paris part-time to finance the domaine while studying viticulture and winemaking. She learned by exchanging with winemakers she admired, such as Henri Milan in Provence and the Clairet family from Domaine de la Tournelle in the Jura. While those encounters

1

1. Winemaker Athénaïs de Béru.

2. Smoke break amidst the Kimmeridgian limestone soil of Chablis.

2

solidified her desire to work naturally, the young vigneronne's return to her native Chablis, a rather chauvinistic hamlet mostly dominated by the sons of great estates, was met with resistance. "Chablis was a really hostile climate for me," she recalls. "I was a woman. I was from Paris. And I wanted to work organically. I was the antithesis of normal."

Chablis is perhaps one of the most heralded wine regions in France. Famous for producing crisp white wines from chardonnay, Burgundy's northernmost vineyards are made up of steep rolling hills where chalky white stones blanket the ground, a sneak peek of an underground world dominated by Kimmeridgian soil (a mix of crushed limestone and marine fossils), the region's calling card for minerality.

"Chablis has become a standardized product," decries Athénaïs, blaming France's AOC system, established in 1935. In theory, the idea to create a set of standards that would safeguard a wine's origins and ensure a winemaker's endeavors were profitable sounds good. Great, even. But in practice, as industrialization began to infiltrate every part of the winemaking process in the 1970s, with liberal use of machinery and chemicals in the vineyard and the cellar, the AOC system evolved to favor mass-production and higher profits over the production of wines that reflected the history and terroir of a given region. "Chablis is one of those well-known appellations that completely rests on its laurels. The demand is so much higher than the offer that Chablis producers don't need to make any efforts to sell their wines," says Athénaïs. "This is unfortunate, because it hinders the evolution of our appellation." Today, the Chablis AOC feels more like a brand name than a quality seal.

In 2006, with fresh eyes on her family's estate and winemaking as a whole, Athénaïs converted the vineyards into organics and then into biodynamics. Results were stark: yields were reduced due to the lack of chemical fertilizers, but the overall quality of the grapes improved, as did the resulting wines. Over the next few years, the young winemaker moved away from what she learned during her oenology studies and began fermenting her wines using only native yeasts, reduced sulfite additions to nearly zero, and forwent chaptalization (the addition of sugar before fermentation is a pervasive process in Chablis because grapes often struggle to ripen due to the region's cooler climate). Athénaïs also started to vinify each parcel individually, resulting in a lineup of distinctive wines that are a testament to the existence of terroir. Stripping wines like Chablis from their usual additives and alterations can reveal unexpected treasures, and when you allow them to go through malolactic fermentation, as they are naturally inclined to do, another level of richness shines through. It's like adding more bass to a tone overwhelmed by treble.

After dropping off our bags in one of the château's opulently decorated rooms, complete with ornate canopy beds and patterned sheets that match the wallpaper, Athénaïs urges us to follow her to Clos de Béru, the domaine's famed walled vineyard. This clos is considered a special place for a reason: its gentle north-facing slopes offer the vines an afternoon kiss of photosynthesis, which in turn provides the wines with an extra level of ripeness. On this night, it is also gracing us with a striking sunset that paints the sky fiery orange. Soon we are met by the live-in harvest team, a mix of Italians, Canadians, and Brooklynites who have all traveled here for a chance to learn from Athénaïs. "It's important for me to exchange with people who share a similar vision of viticulture and winemaking," she says. Over the years, several members of her harvest teams have gone on to start their own winemaking projects, like Marthe Henry (see p.92) in Meursault. Former Noma cook Tess Davison, who was tasked with feeding the domaine's harvest team that year, bought a parcel of vines in the south of France just a few months after our visit. Although Athénaïs has struggled to fit in with the conventional winemakers of Chablis, it's obvious standing here, drinking and chatting with such an eclectic group of people, that she has built her own community of like-minded outsiders.

In the spring of 2016, Athénaïs was reminded, quite brutally, of the importance of the relationships she has built over the years, when black frost and hail destroyed her entire production. Immediately, everyone, from her old mentor Henri Milan to Cyril Fhal at Clos du Rouge Gorge, came to her rescue and offered grapes for her to vinify in Béru, so that she could keep the domaine afloat. "It was was a pivotal year. Now there are wineries all around Chablis that

3. Steph poses for Xavier in Château de Béru while everyone else is hard at work harvesting the 2022 vintage.

4. Château de Béru at night.

5. (Right) Ulysse loves to lounge in Château de Béru's courtyard.

are installing heating cables in the vineyards," explains the winemaker. Mostly running on electricity, these cables meant to prevent frost sometimes have to rely on generators powered by fuel, which goes against Athénaïs' life work. "To me, resorting to that method means we've reached the limit of our profession. Maybe we should just stop and do something else," she says.

Determined to find natural ways to adapt her work to the growing effects of climate change, Athénaïs has been traveling to the South of France to learn about the region's indigenous grape varietals, such as picpoul, terret, and carignan blanc. "There's no miracle answer to climate change, but even in the South, where there are drought problems, these varieties resist," she says. "It's also interesting to learn about local ancestral practices. Maybe they can teach us a better way to work our wines [in Chablis]." This desire to keep learning has led to the creation of Mare Nostrum, a négoce project in the South of France that she operates alongside her husband, Antoine Isenbrandt.

When we visit her in 2022, Athénaïs is in the middle of her seventeenth harvest. Even during the most stressful time of year, she welcomes us with the utmost warmth and engages us in passionate conversations about the future of natural wine, while confidently juggling a staff of thirty people, two young daughters, and a large-scale construction project that will see many areas of the domaine revamped, including the bottling line and a new tasting room. Given how far she's come since moving back to Béru, the winemaker could have very well chosen to fall in line with other winemakers in Chablis and rest on the laurels of what she had built. But why be like everyone else when you can be Athénaïs?

WINERY   FR

6. Harvesters check in with the outside world after the first few hours of harvest, which starts at sunrise.

7. The *casse-croûte*, a smattering of snacks and coffee, is essential fuel for harvesters.

8. *Vive la France!*

7

8

WHOLE ROASTED HARVEST FISH

SERVES 6–8

This recipe is inspired by saucisses au marc de raisin, a traditional harvest dish that uses grape marc or pomace (a combination of grape skins, seeds, and stems that are left after the grapes have been pressed for their juice). Since Athénaïs grows exclusively chardonnay grapes in Chablis, this version—the brainchild of her husband and winemaking partner, Antoine Isenbrandt—swaps sausage and red grapes for whole fish and white grapes. During the cooking process, the grape marc cocoons the fish and imparts its flesh with rich and herbaceous wine aromas. While this recipe is difficult to recreate at home unless you have access to a winery, the result was too beautiful and delicious to keep to ourselves. If you live near a winery, try calling them to see if they can spare a little grape marc and juice around harvest time.

INGREDIENTS

- 2 striped bass (about 2¼ lbs each), cut open and cleaned (ask your fishmonger to do this)
- Salt
- 2 tsp crushed Szechuan peppercorns
- 2 lemons, sliced
- 4 tbs peeled sliced ginger
- 4 tbs chopped chives
- 1 cup fresh herb leaves (we like a mix of sage, parsley, and agastache)
- ¼ cup extra-virgin olive oil
- Black pepper
- 4 lbs white grape marc
- 6 green onions, ends trimmed
- 4 cups fermenting white grape juice

INSTRUCTIONS

1. Preheat the oven to 350°F.

2. Season the fish inside and out with 2 tbs salt and the Szechuan peppercorns. Stuff with a layer of lemon slices, ginger rounds, chives, and fresh herbs. Close each fish, rub the outside with ½ tbs olive oil, and sprinkle with salt and black pepper.

3. In a large Dutch oven, add half of the grape marc, pressing to even it out, to create a layer that's about 2 inches thick. Carefully place both fish on top of the grape marc, seam facing up. Add the green onions around the fish and use the rest of the grape marc to cover everything up. Slowly pour the grape juice over, careful not to add too much to overflow the pot.

4. Cook over medium-high heat and bring to a simmer, about 10 minutes. Transfer the pot to the oven and bake for 35 minutes, or until the internal temperature of the fish reads 145°F.

5. Take the fish out of the oven and transfer to a platter with some of the grape marc. Drizzle with the remaining olive oil and serve immediately.

Les Faverelles

**PATRICK BRINGER &
ISABELLE GEORGELIN**

"You have to be really patient and attentive, and sometimes you have to take a step back, which is never easy," says Isabelle Georgelin. "You also have to stop before it destroys you." While she is referring to the end of her twelve-year tenure as the mayor of Asquins, a small village in Northwestern Burgundy, Isabelle could just as well be talking about her and her husband's journey with Les Faverelles, the winery they started over twenty years ago.

Welcoming us into their home in Asquins, Isabelle is a whirlwind of energy. With her attention already split between the quiche Lorraine in the oven and the sautéed pork with Époisses on the stove, she gives us a quick tour of the house, all while dancing to one of the many CDs in her collection. In contrast, Patrick is tall and stoic, with a bushy mustache that takes up half his face, making his mood hard to read.

Once belonging to Patrick's grandfather, the house is crowded with towering piles of books and an eclectic array of objects and knick-knacks, each more peculiar than the last. On the dining room walls, a collection of masks that seem plucked from the set of *Eyes Wide Shut* stares out at the table as if waiting for us to speak. In one corner of the dining room, a floor lamp stands tall, sporting a lampshade shaped like a gentleman's bowler hat. Finally, in the kitchen, hanging above a shelf precariously stacked with spices, jams, and snacks, a sign reads, "Excusez du désordre mais ici, on vit" (Sorry about the mess, but we live here).

Before moving to Asquins to become a winemaker, Patrick worked as a book merchant in Paris. Seeking a new challenge and a quieter life away from the city, he fondly recalled a time in his early twenties when he worked harvest at

1. (Left) The small shop at Les Faverelles doubles as a hub to welcome clients and as the entrance to the cellar where the wines are made and aged.

2. Life imitates art at lunch with Patrick and Isabelle.

his dad's friend's estate in Champagne. "I would spend all my evenings with the winemaker, and he would show me the ropes," he says. "It always stuck with me."

In 2001, he and Isabelle settled on five and a half acres of mostly chardonnay, pinot noir, and a few vines of césar (an ancient indigenous red varietal). With Vézelay located less than three kilometers away, the couple began making organic wines under the historical town's namesake regional appellation. "When we started, people thought we were crazy," recalls Patrick. "But when they saw pallets of wine being shipped to Japan, they realized we weren't so crazy after all."

Today, Les Faverelles produces distinctive wines, beloved around the world, that exemplify the ability of Northern Burgundy's cold climate to produce low-alcohol wines with refreshing acidity, minerality, and fine tannins. Made with chardonnay, the whites are lean, crisp, and acid-driven—perfect for cutting through Époisses, a rich, creamy, and pungent cheese from the nearby village of the same name. The reds are almost see-through and undeniably easy to drink, and thanks in part to their cold climate roots, they exhibit fresh tannins and cranberry-like tartness.

One of their most popular cuvées, "Le Nez de Muse," made in both white and red wine, is named in honor of their late dog Muse, who loved eating grapes straight from the vine. "She would only eat them when they were ripe, so we would know when it was time to harvest," says Patrick. Since Muse's passing, the couple has welcomed two new dogs, Ollie, who passed away in 2023, and Uzès, both of whom Isabelle jokingly describes as lazy. "They only eat the grapes if they're already cut," she laughs.

Patrick escorts us to the winery, located in the center of the village, in a building so small that the winemaker himself can barely fit through the front door. Once inside, we find ourselves in the stockroom, a small space filled with six-packs of wine, label rolls, and, on a small burner in the corner, a pot of leftover red wax, now dried up, used to dip the tips of wine bottles. We make our way down a steep, cobweb-draped staircase to the cellar, a tiny, medieval underground structure just big enough to fit about 20 barrels—most of which, sadly, appear to be empty. "In 2021, we lost about 80 percent of our production due to frost," explains Patrick.

It's no secret that climate change has been sending shockwaves throughout the wine world, but in the northern reaches of Burgundy, where spring frost has become an increasingly common threat, the situation is especially alarming. In recent decades, rising temperatures have caused plants to bud earlier, making them vulnerable to frost damage and posing a serious risk of losing entire vintages. Winemakers have tried a myriad of techniques to protect their vines, ranging from lighting fires between rows to employing helicopters to circulate warmer air, but they have yet to discover a foolproof solution to the persistent threat of frost.

"For a while, every year was more or less the same, but now it's become complicated from a commercial standpoint because people don't understand why we don't have wine to sell them," says Patrick. This challenge has forced the couple to adapt to the unpredictability of the climate,

3. Winemaker Isabelle Georgelin.

attuning themselves to nature's whims. "Some people say it's empathy—we're attentive to nature and people," says Isabelle. "We're both on the same wavelength about that."

Perhaps due to her time in politics, a period during which she spent years listening to other people's concerns, Isabelle has recently become more introspective about her and Patrick's own needs. As time goes by and the couple ages in conjunction with the intensification of climate change, they have come to realize that maintaining their current operation is untenable. As a result, they've made the tough decision to part with some of their vineyards, with the intention to hold on to Le Clos du Duc, the parcel where they craft La Bise.

Approaching this separation with their characteristic care, they have been meticulously assessing and working with potential successors to ensure they are up to the task. "It's a hard job. You have to be extremely passionate, resilient, and have a lot of character. Otherwise, people are going to eat you alive," remarks Isabelle, once again inadvertently drawing parallels between the demanding nature of winemaking and politics.

3

QUICHE LORRAINE WITH WILD MUSHROOMS

SERVES 8

Growing up, Isabelle's grandfather (a proud man who originated from the Lorraine, the Northeastern French region known for its eponymous quiche) used to bake a great variety of quiches for the family. This recipe, made with wild mushrooms foraged by Isabelle and Patrick and showered with Comté cheese, is the vigneronne's way of keeping her grandfather's memory alive and our bellies satiated.

INGREDIENTS

Dough
Unsalted butter, for greasing the pan
1 cup   spelt flour
1 tsp   salt
½ tsp   black pepper
3½ tbs salted butter, melted

Filling
3 tbs   salted butter
2 cups wild mushrooms, sliced (we like a mix of ceps and trumpets)
½ cup   chopped smoked bacon
7 large eggs
1⅔ cups cream
1 tsp   salt
1 tsp   black pepper
1 tbs   crushed dried marjoram
1 cup   grated Comté cheese

INSTRUCTIONS

1. Preheat the oven to 400°F. Butter a ceramic tart pan and set aside.

2. **For the dough:** In a large bowl, combine the flour, salt, and black pepper. Using your fingertips, blend the melted butter into the flour until it starts to look like coarse sand. Gradually add in about 1 tbs of water and continue mixing until the ingredients come together. Knead until the dough looks smooth and feels elastic. Shape it into a disk, wrap it, and chill in the fridge for 15 minutes.

3. **For the filling:** In a large frying pan over low heat, melt the butter. Add the mushrooms and cook slowly until browned and very tender, about 4 to 5 minutes. Set aside.

4. Roll out the dough and stretch in the buttered tart pan. Scatter the smoked bacon on top, followed by the cooked mushrooms.

5. In a large bowl, whisk the eggs, cream, salt, pepper, and marjoram to combine. Pour the egg mixture over the mushrooms and bacon, and top with the grated Comté cheese. Transfer to the oven and bake for about 35 minutes, until the eggs have settled. Remove from the oven and let it cool down for a few minutes before slicing and serving.

Marthe Henry

Xavier is crouched in the corner of the kitchen, flipping through a pile of records. Every plate has been licked clean and stacked, which should indicate that our dinner at Meursault winemaker Marthe Henry's house is winding down. Except the candles are still burning, we're still laughing, and all of us have that familiar, ok-just-one-more-bottle twinkle in our eyes.

"No way... *Starmania*!" shouts Xavier as he pulls out a twelve-inch vinyl of the 1978 cyberpunk rock opera. "Allez!" chants Marthe's mother, Mijo. Gently, Xavier places the record on the turntable and lowers the stylus. A faint crackling sound is followed by the soft, melodic notes of a piano. Our excitement is palpable. We pass the record sleeve around, passionately debating our favorite songs while doing our best to explain to the few non-native French speakers at the table (cough cough, Zev) why *Starmania* is such a big deal.

Created by French composer Michel Berger and Quebecois lyricist Luc Plamondon, *Starmania* is one of the most enduring French-language musicals. Beyond its ability to capture the human experience in a way that transcends time, borders, and generations, *Starmania* represents a shared experience between France and Quebec, two nations who, despite sharing a language, have often been at odds culturally. The songs are so ubiquitous in both nations that for generations of French and Quebecois adults, including those of us gathered around the table, *Starmania* holds a special place in the soundtrack of our lives.

Moments before Steph has the chance to launch into a rant about Céline Dion's 1991 cover of the *Starmania* song "Un garçon pas comme les autres (Ziggy)," Claude Dubois's voice fills the room. Without skipping a beat, we all start singing "Le Blues du businessman" in unison:

> *"J'ai réussi et j'en suis fier/ Au fond je n'ai qu'un seul regret/J' fais pas ce que j'aurais voulu faire/J'aurais voulu être un artiste"* (I've succeeded and I'm proud of it/But deep down, I only have one regret/I'm not doing what I wanted to do/I would've liked to be an artist)

Watching Marthe belt out these words, Dubois's song about a disillusioned businessman who dreams of leaving everything behind to become an artist takes on a life of its own.

1. Winemaker Marthe Henry.
2. The ever-smiling Mijo, Marthe's mom, takes a break from preparing Gaston Gérard Chicken.

Marthe wasn't always on track to become a winemaker. Born in Paris, she was a bright child who excelled in school. During the summers, her family would visit her grandparents, who were winegrowers in Meursault. (Her grandfather was the well-respected winemaker Pierre Boillot.) Marthe's fascination with winemaking was evident from the start. "It's a bit like Obelix, who fell into the cauldron of magic potion when he was little, you know? I didn't really have a choice," she says, laughing.

Despite her natural inclination, and at her family's suggestion, Marthe put her winemaking aspirations on the back burner to focus on her journalism studies. But even after years of working as a television reporter, the idea of starting over as a winemaker lingered. "I thought, instead of sitting there waiting for a midlife crisis, I could just go through it in my thirties."

In 2013, Marthe moved into the family home in Meursault and went back to school, this time in viticulture and oenology. By 2017, after spending a few years working at neighboring Domaine Rougeot, she embarked on her own winemaking journey by purchasing grapes and vinifying them in the family cellar. Through mutual connections, she formed a close bond with the iconoclastic Chablis winemaker Athénaïs de Béru (p.78), who saw in Marthe a younger version of herself. "I took her under my wing, because I could see that she was also going to be faced with similar challenges I encountered when I started," says Athénaïs. Like Chablis in the north, the culture of Meursault is rather chauvinistic. This made it difficult for Marthe to combat the prejudices held by old-school winemakers against her. Despite being perceived as nothing but an inexperienced woman from Paris attempting to make natural wine, the determined young winemaker persisted.

Famous for producing full-bodied, buttery, and age-worthy white wines primarily from chardonnay grapes, Meursault isn't particularly popular with natural-wine crowds who favor brighter, easy-drinking wines. But Marthe's wines, although classical in style, exude vitality and a stripped-down quality that sets them apart from those of her neighbors. "I strive to produce wines that express terroir as transparently as possible," says Marthe. "Wines that aren't overpowered by *élevage*, in which you can't feel the winemaker's touch."

In the coming years, Marthe hopes to recover some of her grandparents' vines to cultivate her own grapes. "I don't want hectares upon hectares of vines. I don't want to make a billion bottles. My goal is to continue managing everything on my own, from tending to the vineyard and cellar, to bottling and marketing," she explains.

Back in Marthe's kitchen, "Le Blues du businessman" is drawing to a close:

3

J'aurais voulu être un artiste/ Pour pourvoir dire pourquoi j'existe
(I would've liked to be an artist/To be able to say why I exist)

Marthe is beaming. Unlike *Starmania*'s businessman, she is finally living her lifelong dream. In this very moment, it becomes clear to us that the young winemaker's daring spirit could make just about anything old feel new again, whether it's wine from an appellation like Meursault or a musical from the late 1970s.

WINERY

3. Marthe puts on the vinyl of *Starmania*, much to Steph's and Xav's delight.

4. Marthe passes a bucket of healthy-looking pinot noir.

4

GASTON GÉRARD CHICKEN

SERVES 4-6

This classic Burgundian dish was created by accident by the wife of the former Mayor of Dijon, Gaston Gérard. The story goes that in 1930, the couple was set to host Curnonsky, one of the twentieth century's most celebrated French food writers. As Madame was preparing a chicken dish for the occasion, she accidentally sprinkled too much paprika, overpowering the rest of the ingredients. In order to fix her mistake and prevent utter embarrassment, she added crème fraîche and white wine to balance out the spice. The result was a rich and comforting chicken dish that instantly won over one of the country's toughest critics. The recipe remains a crowd pleaser to this day—especially when paired with a glass of Marthe's chardonnay.

INGREDIENTS

- 1 whole chicken (about 3½ lbs), cut into 8 pieces
- Salt and black pepper
- 4 tbs extra-virgin olive oil
- 2 tbs salted butter
- 3 medium shallots, chopped
- ½ bottle of dry white wine (about 12.7 oz), preferably chardonnay
- 2 cups heavy cream
- 4 tbs Dijon mustard
- 1 tsp sweet paprika
- 1 cup grated Comté cheese

INSTRUCTIONS

1. Preheat the oven to 400°F.

2. Pat the chicken pieces dry and season with salt and pepper. Heat a large Dutch oven over medium-high heat, then add the oil and butter. Once the butter has melted, add the chicken pieces and sear until lightly colored, 3 to 4 minutes on each side. Remove and set aside.

3. Reduce the heat to medium and add the shallots. Cook until translucent, about 3 to 5 minutes. Stir in the white wine, cream, mustard, and paprika. Return the seared chicken pieces to the Dutch oven and bring to a simmer. Cover the pot and cook until the chicken is almost cooked through, about 35 minutes.

4. Sprinkle the grated Comté cheese over the chicken and transfer to the oven, uncovered. Bake for 10 to 15 minutes, until the chicken is cooked through, and a light crust has formed. Serve immediately.

GRANDMOTHER'S CRÈME CARAMEL

SERVES 1

Every time they come over for dinner, Marthe's friends request her grandmother's classic crème caramel. After enjoying it ourselves at the end of our meal with the Henry family, it's easy to understand why. Since the quality of dairy and eggs is so different in France than in North America, due to stricter regulations, David gracefully adapted Marthe's family recipe for home cooks, and after getting a taste of it at the end of a long day at his farm, we can attest it's just as good as the original.

INGREDIENTS

- **1 cup** sugar
- **½ cup** whole milk
- **6** large eggs
- **2** cans condensed milk (14 oz each)
- **2** cans evaporated milk (12 oz each)
- **1** vanilla bean, split and scraped

INSTRUCTIONS

1. Preheat the oven to 325°F.

2. In a heavy-bottomed saucepan set over medium-high heat, add the sugar and just enough water to cover. Heat until the mixture reaches a soft boil and becomes dark golden brown, almost like a dark maple syrup, about 6 to 8 minutes. Adjust the heat as needed, raising to avoid sugar crystals from forming on the side of the pot, lowering if it's burning on the side. Once ready, quickly pour the caramel into a Charlotte mold and set aside to harden.

3. In a medium bowl, add the milk, eggs, condensed and evaporated milks, and vanilla bean and whisk to combine. Pour the mixture over the hardened caramel. Place the Charlotte mold in a large ovenproof pot and fill the pot with water until it reaches halfway up the mold. Bake for 40 minutes, or until the edges have set but the center is still slightly shaky. (It should be a tight jiggle!) Cover and refrigerate until completely cooled, about 2 hours.

Domaine Chandon de Briailles

FRANÇOIS & CLAUDE DE NICOLAY

1. Winemaker François de Nicolay.
2. Steph finds another way to avoid harvesting by preparing a large salad for the crew at Chandon de Briailles.
3. Generations of de Nicolay on display.

It takes a minute for our eyes to adjust to the darkness. François de Nicolay, who runs Chandon de Briailles alongside his sister Claude, is guiding us through the cellar that lies beneath the domaine's eighteenth-century château. Despite the dim lighting and the unavoidable sensorial fatigue that comes with embarking on our umpteenth cellar visit of the year, our eyes are immediately drawn to the ornate columns that grace the space. When we point out the incongruity of having such intricately designed support beams in an otherwise utilitarian room filled with rows of stacked oak barrels and unlabeled bottles, François answers softly without pretense, "Ah yes, well this room was actually designed by Gustave Eiffel." Yes, *that* Eiffel.

While impressive, this fact is a lot less shocking once you know that Count and Countess de Briailles are the official titles of the siblings. Even the perfectly manicured French-style gardens that surround the château are said to have been designed by the team behind the Gardens of Versailles. But the family's illustrious connections stretch far beyond design. Their ancestor Pierre-Gabriel Chandon, who married Jean-Rémy Moët's daughter in the 1800s, is the cofounder of the famed champagne house Moët-Chandon. In more recent history, François and Claude can count none other than Jacques Guerlain, one of the most prolific and influential perfumers of the twentieth century, as their great-granduncle.

By now, you've probably realized that the story of Chandon de Briailles is not your typical natural-wine tale. Established in 1834, the domaine remained rather unknown until François and Claude's mother, Nadine de Nicolay, took over in 1982. She was the first to bottle and sell wine under the domaine name instead of selling unfinished barrels to the *négociants* of Beaune, as was customary. In the late 1980s, Nadine put an end to the use of pesticides and herbicides in the vineyards and started treating the vines with an old-school *bouillie* bordelaise (a copper sulfate mix used as a fungicide), as well as working the soil using tractors and plows.

In 2001, François received a call from his mother. At the time, the young man was living in Paris where he owned and operated a small wine shop called Pinot Noir et Chardonnay. "She told me she was tired and that she wanted to retire," he recalls. However, Nadine didn't want to leave Claude, who had been working with her since 1990, with the burden of managing the domaine on her own. She wanted François to take over Chandon de Briailles with his sister. "I thought about it for about ten minutes and then I made a few phone calls and sold my shop in Paris," he adds.

Influenced by the natural wines François had grown fond of in Paris, the siblings started

1

converting their vineyards to biodynamic agriculture. They eventually ditched the use of tractors and bought a few horses to work the soil. "There's a bit of everything in the world of natural wines," says François. "But I'm especially drawn to wines that reflect their terroir. And here in Burgundy, terroir is everything."

As discussed in the introduction to this chapter (p.74), Burgundy's appellation system is rooted in the concept of terroir, emphasizing the unique traits of specific vineyards and their impact on a wine's taste. While this system has contributed to Burgundy's global recognition and economic success, it has been undermined by the advent of modern winemaking techniques that allow for extensive adjustments to a wine's taste and texture, often severing its connection to terroir. Despite this, certain heavily manipulated grand cru wines continue to sell at a premium. This means that there is very little economic incentive for a Burgundian winemaker to make the often-costly transition to natural winemaking.

"Taking risks is scary for a lot of people given the level of appellations and prices in the region," says François. "People are afraid of making mistakes, and they think if they mess up with a wine in an appellation like Chambolle, they'll be in deep trouble."

While adopting natural viticulture and winemaking comes with genuine financial risks, such as lower grape yields, increased labor costs, and unpredictable results, these risks can be minimized by following a gradual approach, as demonstrated by François and Claude at Chandon de Briailles. "We did it little by little. It's a process that took fifteen years or so. It can't be done all at once," says the winemaker.

In parallel to Chandon de Briailles, François started an eponymous négoce project, sourcing organic grapes from entry-level

2

3

4. (Left) A truck loaded with bins of pinot noir and topped with an open bottle, parked on the side of the road in Savigny-lès-Beaune.

5. They say that the experience of working harvest really stays with you, but so do the spiky little burrs that cling to your clothes.

6. François and Claude de Nicolay reflect, projecting comfort during yet another harvest of some of the most sought-after wines of the world.

5

6

Burgundy appellations like Côte de Beaune and Mercurey. "It allows me to make wines that are a little less expensive and easier to access," he says. "Some of my favorite wine bars wouldn't necessarily buy Chandon wines because they're too expensive, but they can afford François de Nicolay."

Beyond the alluring price point, the négoce project allows François more freedom to experiment with no-sulfur winemaking. "If I take a risk and fail, it's my own thing. It's not associated with my family," he explains, adding that the experiments from his négoce project have informed his winemaking at Chandon de Briailles.

Despite his success, the winemaker remains cautious with anything that touches Chandon de Briailles. "We have to keep both parties happy," he says. "But little by little, we've managed to bring this estate, which is very much anchored in the old classical world, into the world of natural wines." In 2021, 90 percent of the domaine's production was made without sulfur, proving that natural wine doesn't automatically mean young, funky, and cloudy. Natural wine can also mean terroir-driven, rich, textured chardonnay from an eighteenth-century Burgundian estate.

As we emerge from the cellar, our eyes immediately land on a group of construction workers busy fixing up the stones on the second floor of the château. They're working slowly and meticulously, just like François and Claude, not to transform the estate but simply to restore and honor what came before them.

BOEUF BOURGUIGNON

SERVES 4–6

A historic Burgundian recipe for a historic Burgundian estate. What more could you ask for? Every harvest season, the de Nicolay family feeds their team with dishes typical of the region. The reason is simple, according to François. "Several of our harvesters come from other countries and want to discover our regional cuisine," he says. To successfully recreate this recipe, make sure you use a good red wine—it doesn't need to be Chandon de Briailles Corton Grand Cru, but keep in mind that its flavor will infuse the entire dish.

INGREDIENTS

Bouquet Garni
4 sprigs thyme
6 sprigs parsley
2 bay leaves
Cheesecloth
Butcher's twine

Boeuf Bourguignon
3½ tbs salted butter
2 tbs extra-virgin olive oil
1 medium white onion, roughly chopped
1 cup lardons (or diced bacon)
3⅓ lbs beef chuck (or other boneless stewing beef), cut into 2-inch cubes
½ cup all-purpose flour
1 bottle red Burgundy wine (25.4 oz)
2 cups beef broth
1 garlic clove, smashed
1 tbs salt
1 tsp black pepper

To Finish
2 carrots, chopped like wine corks
1 celery heart, quartered
1 cup celery root chunks
2 cups pearl onions
Extra-virgin olive oil
Salt and black pepper
2 cups white button mushrooms

INSTRUCTIONS

1. **For the bouquet garni:** Place the herbs in the center of a square of cheesecloth. Gather up the corners to close it like a package. Tie it securely using butcher's twine.

2. **For the boeuf bourguignon:** In a large Dutch oven, melt the butter with the oil over medium-low heat. Add the onion and lardons and cook until golden, about 6 to 8 minutes. Transfer to a bowl and set aside.

3. Reduce the heat to medium, then add the beef cubes to the Dutch oven and cook until browned. Sprinkle with the flour and stir to coat. Keep cooking until the flour takes on a golden color, about 5 minutes. Pour in the red wine and stir to remove any bits that have stuck to the bottom of the pot. Add in the beef broth, return the cooked onion and lardons to the pot, and add the smashed garlic, salt, pepper, and bouquet garni. Turn the heat up to high and bring to a boil, stirring occasionally. Cover and reduce the heat to low. Simmer for 3 hours, or until the beef is fork-tender.

4. **To finish:** Once you are 2 hours in on the beef braising, preheat the oven to 300°F. Scatter the carrots, celery heart, celery root, and pearl onions onto a large baking sheet. Drizzle with olive oil and sprinkle with salt and pepper. Transfer to the oven and roast for 30 to 40 minutes, until the vegetables are fork-tender with brown edges.

5. Add the mushrooms to the Dutch oven and remove the bouquet garni. Continue cooking for another 30 minutes, until you've reached the 3-hour mark. (If you notice the sauce is too thick, add some water.) Serve in your favorite country bowl and decorate with the roasted vegetables on top. Serve with mashed potatoes, fresh tagliatelle (p. 212), or a loaf of bread for dipping.

FR   WINERY

Maison en Belles Lies

PIERRE & MICHÈLE FENALS

1

There are two types of people in life: those who insist that you can't teach an old dog new tricks and those who believe that you're never too old to embrace change. The former tend to be closed-off, convinced that once we settle into our ways, change becomes impossible. Conversely, the latter group welcomes new opportunities with open arms—a sentiment mirrored by winemaker Pierre Fenals and his wife, Michèle, the moment we step through the wide-open doors of their charming stone house, nestled in a lush corner of Saint-Aubin.

With a warm smile and sporting bold red rounded eyeglasses, Pierre exudes the monk-like zen of someone who embraces the ever-changing nature of life. Born in Algeria, Pierre pursued molecular biochemistry studies in Marseille and worked in pharmaceutical laboratories before building a successful career as a store developer in the textile industry in Paris. Then, in 1985, a serendipitous find at a flea market altered the course of his life. The discovery? A book by Rudolf Steiner, recognized by many as the founder of biodynamic agriculture. While Pierre's scientific and marketing background anchored him in hard data, Steiner's teachings urged him to consider the life forces and natural elements of the land.

"My father-in-law owned a farm, and that's where we conducted our initial biodynamic experiments," Pierre recalls. "Through this process, I connected with winemakers and market gardeners in the Loire and Alsace who shared similar principles, introducing me to the world of natural wine."

In their fifties, when most people would start hashing out retirement plans, Pierre and Michèle were contemplating a late-career shift. Crushed by the pressure of living in the city, they considered buying an old building in the countryside to open a B&B with an adjoining restaurant and an artist residency. "We had a house and a few friends in Burgundy, so we decided to settle here instead," Pierre reflects. "While I knew a lot about wine, my understanding of viticulture was limited, so I decided to study viticulture in Beaune and oenology in Dijon."

2

1. Whole clusters of pinot noir macerate and begin fermentation in these large-size tronconic wooden vats in the Maison en Belles Lies winery.

2. Pierre opens up a bottle while Michèle prepares a snack at the winery.

3. Pierre gets the ham steak ready for the oven.

In school, Pierre crossed paths with Mathieu Lapierre, son of Marcel Lapierre, one of the godfathers of the natural-wine movement. Following graduation, Pierre spent seven years gaining experience at various wineries, ranging from large-scale conventional facilities to biodynamic vineyards like Domaine Emmanuel Giboulot and Trapet Père et Fils in Burgundy.

In 2009, after acquiring vines in Santenay, Monthelie, and Corton, Pierre began producing wines under the label Maison en Belles Lies, a name inspired by a correspondence between seventeenth-century monks from Tuscany and Cîteaux. "The Tuscan monks discerned that by racking the red wines and retaining only the fine lees (*belles lies*), or sediments, they could develop finer aromas and prolong shelf life. They shared this technique with the monks of Cîteaux for their grand crus," explains Pierre.

Despite their classical profiles, the vast majority of Pierre's wines are crafted with no additives whatsoever. The white wines undergo sufficient barrel ageing (at least one year) to achieve clarity and precision, yet some retain a touch of cloudiness, which in turn enhances texture and provides protection against oxidation. The reds pack a moderate tannic grip while maintaining a lean character, and co-fermented cuvées like L'Étrange (crafted from pinot noir, gamay, and chardonnay) make for the perfect feather-light, fruity chilled red.

Back in Saint-Aubin, the aroma of roasting pork drifts into the backyard through the open windows of the house. Listening to Pierre speak amidst the natural soundtrack of chirping birds and buzzing bees feels like we just pressed play on a meditation tape. "I love working with vines. They're living organisms thriving in living soil, surrounded by animals and birds," he muses softly. "Wine, too, is alive. Throughout fermentation and ageing, it moves. It has a life force. Here, among nature, you're more intimately connected

3

to the living than you could ever be in the city." It's evident that the suffocating grip of urban life, once dreaded by Pierre and Michèle, is far behind them.

Regarding the future of the domaine as the couple ages, Pierre doesn't seem to worry much about that either. "I'm an old man, you know. Maybe I'll ease up a bit, and instead of producing fifty thousand bottles, I'll cut that in half," he says. In recent years, the winemaker has started leasing vines to some of his former collaborators, who now bottle under their own labels. Perhaps Pierre will find someone interested in taking over the domaine, or maybe Maison en Belles Lies, as we know it today, will gradually fade away alongside Pierre and Michèle, making room for another project to rise from its ashes. Regardless, more than two decades since taking the leap into winemaking, the couple remains as open as ever to life's possibilities. "It's our way of life. For instance, at our house, the door's always open. We don't have a key anyway," Pierre chuckles.

4

WINERY   FR

5

6

4. Winemaker Pierre Fenals outside his home in Saint-Aubin.

5. Pierre and Michèle serve lunch at the winery.

6. A collection of cartoons displayed on Pierre and Michèle's fridge.

SLOW-COOKED PORK WITH WHITE WINE AND ROOT VEGETABLES

SERVES 6–8

During harvest, days at the domaine tend to be long and exhausting. That is why Pierre and Michèle insist on feeding the entire crew a substantial lunch every single day. For our visit, the Maison en Belles Lies vignerons prepared a typical harvest meal (a feast would be a more accurate description), which consisted of a green salad, dauphinoise potatoes, this slow-cooked pork recipe, a chocolate cake, a Fresh Plum Tart (p. 112), and, of course, cheeses.

INGREDIENTS

- 4 **lbs** fresh ham steak (2 inches thick)
- Salt and black pepper
- 2 **tbs** salted butter
- 1 **tsp** extra-virgin olive oil
- 6 small onions, roughly chopped
- 1 head garlic, cloves peeled and smashed
- 3 **cups** dry white wine
- 4 sprigs thyme
- 1 sprig rosemary
- 4 carrots, roughly chopped
- 4 large yellow-fleshed potatoes, roughly diced
- 2 **tbs** Dijon mustard
- 1 **cup** heavy cream

INSTRUCTIONS

1. Pat the ham steak dry with a paper towel. Season generously with salt and pepper.

2. In a large Dutch oven, heat the butter and oil over medium heat. Once the butter has melted, add the ham steak and sear until golden, about 3 minutes each side. Add the onion and garlic. Cook until fragrant and the alliums have started to soften, about 5 minutes. Stir in the white wine, thyme, and rosemary. Add enough cold water to fully cover the ham and allow the mixture to come to a simmer. Add the carrots and reduce the heat to low. Cover and simmer for 1½ hours.

3. Add the potatoes and mustard to the Dutch oven and stir to combine. Cover and continue cooking until the potatoes are fork-tender, another 30 minutes. Lower the heat to medium-low and and stir in the heavy cream, letting the mixture simmer until the sauce coats the back of a spoon. Serve immediately.

FRESH PLUM TART

MAKES ONE 12-INCH TART

During our visit in early September, Mirabelle plums (a yellow-fleshed and sweet variety of plum commonly cultivated around Nancy in France and Metz in Germany) were in season. Since the fruit's season is fairly short, we felt somewhat blessed to taste a classic Mirabelle tart, even though we were a couple hundred miles from its birthplace in the Lorraine. Don't stress if you can't find Mirabelles where you live; you can recreate this simple tart using ripe golden plums.

INGREDIENTS

- 2⅓ **cups** whole wheat flour
- 1 large egg
- Pinch of salt
- ¼ **cup** sugar
- ¾ **cup (1½ sticks)** unsalted room temperature butter, plus additional for greasing the pan
- 20 plums, halved and pitted

INSTRUCTIONS

1. Preheat the oven to 350°F and butter a 12-inch ceramic tart pan.

2. Pour the flour onto a long piece of parchment paper. Shape the flour into a well and place the egg, salt, sugar, and butter in the center. Using a fork, slowly incorporate the flour into the egg and butter mixture, beating gently until it becomes a messy paste. Knead the dough until it is soft and homogenous. Shape it into a disk and cover it with a second piece of parchment paper. Let it rest for 5 to 8 minutes.

3. With the parchment paper still on top of the dough, roll out the dough until you achieve a circle with a 12-inch diameter. Remove the top piece of parchment, then, keeping the bottom piece of parchment paper, carefully transfer the dough to the tart pan and press firmly against the pan.

4. Transfer to the oven and bake for 5 to 10 minutes, until the dough has become somewhat firm. Remove the dough from the oven and arrange the plums slices on top with some overlap. Return to the oven and bake for 25 to 30 minutes, until golden brown. Let the tart cool slightly before serving.

Maison Valette

PHILIPPE & CÉCILE VALETTE

We conveniently time our arrival to harvest one of Maison Valette's parcels in Pouilly-Fuissé with the mid-morning *casse-croûte*, a break where harvesters relax and refuel with an assortment of snacks that often include savory cakes, hard-boiled eggs, charcuterie, coffee, and, in this case, much to our delight, a few unlabeled bottles of the domaine's Mâcon-Villages chardonnay.

"You got here at the perfect time," says Philippe Valette before letting his trademark raspy laughter resonate all the way up the hill where the winery's famed Clos du Monsieur Noly vineyard is located. "Go on, help yourselves," he adds, pointing us toward the spread laid out on a fold-out plastic table a few feet away. Not only does showing up at this time happily make up for the fact that we skipped breakfast that morning, but it also allows us to mingle with the harvest team, a mix of people from neighboring villages and restaurant-industry kids working in Lyon and Paris, who seem just as excited as we are to work alongside one of the most widely revered figures in natural wine.

Once in the vines and with secateurs in hand, Zev naturally gravitates toward Philippe, hoping to absorb every ounce of the vigneron's wisdom as he openly shares his thoughts on winemaking and vine biology. "Oidium can be a big problem," says the winemaker. He pauses for a moment. "But I'm happy to have a bit of it around because it also carries bacteria and yeasts that can help our fermentations, which have struggled in recent years," he adds, extrapolating on a common fungal infection responsible for drying out grapes.

Saying that harvest is a stressful time is an understatement. In just a matter of days, an entire year's worth of work is at stake, and winemakers only get one shot at doing it right. Unpredictable weather patterns can pose challenges outside anybody's control, but a single man-made mistake can cause enough damage to ruin an entire vintage. Yet, on this unseasonably warm morning in the middle of the 2022 harvest, Philippe appears uncommonly calm. He moves through each row, cutting grape bunches with purpose while also taking time to answer everyone's questions with depth and nuance. What becomes clear in that moment is the Valette family's secret to building great relationships and making even better wines: time.

Maison Valette is run by the warm and playful husband-and-wife duo Philippe and Cécile Valette who, despite knowing each other since childhood, only became an item after decades of friendship. "We went to school together when we were little," says Cécile, who at eight years old moved to Chaintré, a small village on

1. A rainbow stretches over Chaintré, in the Mâconnais.

2. Philippe Valette examines the crux of his life's work: chardonnay.

2

the border of the Mâconnais and the Beaujolais where Philippe's family has been growing grapes for three generations. Philippe always knew he would become a winemaker. Cécile, on the other hand, went off to college in the South of France, where she squandered her time partying until a friend persuaded her to get a degree in wine commerce (her cohort included winemakers Thierry Puzelat, Jean-François Nicq, and Pierre Beauger). Whenever she would go back to Chaintré, Cécile would pay a visit to her longtime friend Philippe Valette. "He was already a winemaker, so I would bring him different things to taste. I also introduced him to my classmates," she says. "That really brought us closer." When they were thirty years old, the two friends became lovers, and shortly after they welcomed the first of their three children, Joséphine; Gaspard and Rose are their other two.

For several years, Cécile kept her job at the INAO (the organization that regulates French agricultural products, like wine, with Protected Designations of Origin) to keep the family afloat, while Philippe pushed his winemaking further. Having already converted the vineyards to organics and introduced biodynamic preparations with the help of his father, Gérard, and brother, Baptiste, in the early nineties, Philippe started experimenting with fermentations that avoided the addition of yeasts and enzymes. While these experiments are considered natural-wine no-brainers nowadays, very few people dared making wine without additives at the time, especially in the Mâconnais, a region historically dominated by large commercial wineries specializing in young, cheap wines that lacked the pedigree of their neighbors to the north in the Côte d'Or.

Simultaneously, and once again going against the grain, Philippe began to lengthen the élevage of his wines, allowing his wines to ferment and age in barrels anywhere from two years for entry-level Mâcon-Villages and up to twelve years for oxidative cuvées like Clos du Monsieur Noly and Clos Reyssier. The resulting wines display levels of richness, depth, and texture that surpass some of the most famous wines of the Côte d'Or. "I think that really the most important part of perfecting the type of wine we make is taking time into account," says Cécile. "But time has a power that we have unfortunately put aside, because today time is money."

This is something the couple had to learn the hard way in 2007, when the bank demanded that they bottle their 2003 vintage in order to pay back a loan they had taken. Philippe and Cécile both knew the wine needed more time to complete its fermentation, with about three to four grams of sugar left to process. But they had no choice. As they feared, three months after bottling, the wines began to referment in the bottles, and they were forced to put them back in barrels, which cost them even more money than if they had just waited.

"It reminds me of a line that's written on a barrel at the Cantillon brewery in Brussels: 'Time does not respect what is done without it,' meaning if you take time to do something, time will respect it," Cécile says. "As a result, we've now completely freed ourselves from releasing vintages consecutively. We're going to bottle the 2019 before the 2018 because each vintage evolves according to its own timeline."

In the early days, making natural wine in the Mâconnais was a lonely experience. Luckily, their endeavors coincided with some of the very first natural-wine fairs that began popping up all over France in the late nineties and early aughts. Any winemaker who was around at the time will gladly tell you, with a nostalgic twinkle in their eye, how magical those early salons were.

"You know, it's this little group of natural winemakers, the first ones at La Dive, the first ones at Le Vin de Mes Amis in Montpellier, those are the people we exchanged with the most because we had the time," says Cécile. A wine fair where winemakers like Philippe and Cécile Valette are free to roam for hours to engage in deep conversations with like-minded winemakers, such as their southern counterparts Charlotte and Jean-Baptiste Sénat (see p.164) is hard to imagine for those of us who only know the modern iteration of those fairs, where long lines, crowded stands, and rushed tastings are the norm. "Those encounters were really important for us because it helped us stand firm in our beliefs. We knew we were the only ones in our region to work naturally, but we knew that elsewhere, there were people doing the same," says Cécile.

The Valette philosophy on taking your time goes beyond falling in love and making great wine. They also pride themselves in the time they invest in the people who work with them. Some of their former apprentices have included Olivier Cohen and Maxime Magnon, who makes incredible wines in Corbières.

"It's hard to convince people in the Mâconnais to work naturally because it means less money. We don't have any external signs of wealth like most people who make conventional wine in Burgundy," says Cécile. "Our wealth is the time

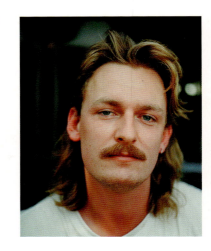

3. Harvester Lohann Barrier.

4. Harvester Jules Delbard.

5. Winemaker Philippe Valette.

6. Our friend and fellow harvester, Calla Camero.

7. (Right) Cécile Valette's aunt Marie-Thé sits in front of a plate of chicken curry with raita.

we get to spend with our friends, colleagues, clients, people we know all over the world, and those who share our vision."

The sun is long gone by the time we gather around long communal tables to enjoy a meal prepared by Cécile, her mother, and Philippe's mother, who is celebrating her fiftieth harvest. Flanked by their children and a few harvesters (or her *loup-loups*, as Cécile affectionately calls them), the Valettes are beaming. Looking around it becomes clear to us, as we share bottles of the best chardonnay in the world with the very people who made it, all under the guise of a book that we're writing with some of our best friends, that we may never feel as rich as we do in this very moment.

WINERY FR

8. Clockwise from bottom left: Steph, Zev, Marie-Thé, Josette Valette, and our friend Josh Fontaine refuel before going back out into the vineyards.

9. Marie-Thé prepares a large batch of onion soup for the harvest team.

10. Cécile and Philippe's son, Gaspard Valette, feeds one of winemaker Olivier Cohen's lambs, which will eventually grow up to wander around the vineyards and mow the lawn.

10

MÂCONNAIS ONION SOUP

SERVES 6

With its deep, savory broth, the sweetness of caramelized onions, and the delightful contrast of the melted cheese and crispy bread, French onion soup is perhaps the ultimate comfort food. A longtime staple in rural communities where onions were abundant and affordable, the soup became a favorite among working-class Parisians in the eighteenth century before being popularized in the United States by chef Julia Child. Nowadays, variations of the classic French onion soup can be found around the world. This recipe, which we enjoyed during our visit, isn't baked like most classic French onion soups. Instead, it receives a shower of freshly grated Comté that slowly melts into the soup as you eat it.

INGREDIENTS

Soup
- ½ cup (1 stick) salted butter
- 6 cups roughly chopped yellow onions
- 2 tbs all-purpose flour
- ⅔ cup dry white wine, preferably chardonnay
- 4½ cups beef broth
- Black pepper
- 1 tsp thyme

Croutons
- 6 slices stale bread, cut into 1-inch cubes
- 2 tbs salted butter, melted
- Salt

To Finish
- 2 cups grated Comté cheese

INSTRUCTIONS

1. Preheat the oven to 400°F.

2. **For the soup:** In a Dutch oven, melt the butter over low heat. Add the onions and cook slowly, stirring every so often to avoid sticking, until the onions have colored slightly but have not burned, about 30 minutes. Sprinkle the onions with the flour and stir to coat. Add the wine and stir to release any bits of onion that have stuck to the bottom of the pot. Pour in the beef broth and a pinch of pepper and thyme. Bring the soup to a simmer on medium-low, and cook for 20 minutes.

3. **For the croutons:** Meanwhile, place the bread cubes in a large bowl and drizzle with the melted butter. Toss until the cubes are nicely coated. Sprinkle with salt and toss again. Scatter the bread cubes on a baking sheet in a single layer. Bake for about 3 minutes, until the croutons are golden. Remove from the oven and set aside.

4. **To finish:** Divide the soup into bowls and top with the freshly baked croutons and grated Comté cheese. Serve immediately.

ÎLE FLOTTANTE

SERVES 6

Originally called *omelette à la neige* (snow omelet) in reference to the fluffy snow-like appearance of the meringue, île flottante (floating island) has a lengthy history that dates back to the seventeenth century. (It is said to have been a favorite dessert of the French royal court during the reign of King Louis XIV.) The beloved dessert can now be found in many culinary traditions worldwide. The Austrians know it as *Schneenockerln* (snow dumplings) and the Italians as *uova di neve* (snow eggs). Whatever you call it, this classic dessert of poached meringues in custard holds a special place in our hearts, especially after enjoying it during harvest in the Mâconnais.

INGREDIENTS

Caramel
1 cup sugar

Île Flottante
6 large eggs
⅔ cup sugar
Seeds from 1 vanilla pod
8 cups milk, plus additional for poaching
Butter biscuits (optional)

INSTRUCTIONS

1. **For the caramel:** Pour the sugar into a small pot with ½ cup of water. Cook over medium heat, stirring often to avoid sticking, until the sugar has melted and turned into a caramel, about 6 to 8 minutes. Set aside.

2. **For the île flottante:** Crack and separate the egg whites and yolks into two large bowls. Add ⅓ cup sugar to the egg yolks and whisk to a creamy consistency. Transfer the mixture to a pot, add the vanilla seeds, and pour in 2 cups of milk. Gently heat over medium heat, whisking constantly, until the custard is thick enough to coat a spoon, about 5 minutes. Set aside.

3. In a medium pot set over medium heat, add 6 cups of milk and bring to a simmer. In a large bowl, using a whisk or an electric mixer, whisk the egg whites until stiff. Gradually add the remaining ⅓ cup sugar and continue whisking until shiny peaks form. Using a large spoon, transfer ⅙ of the meringue mixture to the pot of simmering milk, one by one. Cover and poach until the meringues are firm, 5 to 8 minutes. Remove one at a time with a slotted spoon and set aside on a plate.

4. Divide the custard among 6 bowls and top each with a meringue. Drizzle with caramel and serve with butter biscuits, if desired.

Auvergne

Nestled in the middle of the country and flanked by the Beaujolais to the east, the Auvergne is the site of geological turmoil, as evidenced by the numerous dormant volcanoes that punctuate the region's verdant landscape. (The Chaîne des Puys alone counts eighty volcanoes spread over roughly twenty miles.) In recent years, it has made a name for itself beyond its stunning landscapes by slowly becoming one of France's most sought-after wine-producing regions, despite the near decimation of its vineyards a few centuries ago.

No Pompei-size seismic event is to blame in this case. Rather, an insect about the size of a lentil is responsible for single-handedly destroying most of the European vineyards starting in the mid-nineteenth century. A small aphid that feeds on the roots and leaves of grapevines, phylloxera was brought over from America through imported rootstocks (*Vitis labrusca*). While American grapevine species had evolved to adapt to phylloxera, European grapevines (*Vitis vinifera*) had little to no natural resistance to the pest and suffered severe damage. By the late nineteenth century, it is estimated that up to two-thirds of the vineyard surface in France was lost to phylloxera (some regions lost as much as 90 percent of their vines). Beyond the statistics, it is hard to fully grasp the extent of the economic and cultural impacts of the phylloxera crisis. Several grape varietals went extinct during that time, taking with them tastes, textures, and aromas we will never know. Now, centuries later, much of the European vineyards have been restored by grafting European grapevines onto phylloxera-resistant American rootstocks. However, as a result of the crisis, some regions abandoned their winemaking roots in favor of industrial agriculture. The Auvergne is among them.

At its peak, before the phylloxera crisis, the region counted a little over 43,000 hectares of vines, much of it draped over lower volcano slopes. Today that number is closer to 800 hectares, partly thanks to a small group of forward-thinking natural vignerons who brought the region's winemaking traditions back from near extinction. In the 1990s, enticed by affordable land prices and the thrill of starting a movement from scratch, winemakers like Jean Maupertuis and Patrick Bouju began to make wine using the Auvergne's many grape varietals.

The great majority of wines coming out of the region today are red wines made using a local gamay clone, simply known as gamay d'Auvergne, which exhibits a denser and more electric fruit quality than the gamay wines from neighboring Beaujolais, as well as some pinot noir. The region's modest white wine production is dominated by chardonnay, imprinted with a characteristic and delicate white-mushroom quality, along with some pinot gris, sauvignon blanc, and other misfit varieties. Part of the Auvergne's beauty is the clean slate it offers winemakers. Since there are no old-school estates leading the way, this new generation is virtually free to make up its own rules as it goes.

In this section, you will meet Patrick Bouju, as well as Vincent and Marie Tricot, whose playful dedication put the Auvergne on the map and helped shape the region's boundary-pushing identity at a time when a future had yet to be imagined. Their recipes, using simple local produce that can readily be substituted to match your preferences, mirror the region's unrestrained and free-spirited essence.

FR

Domaine la Bohème

PATRICK BOUJU & JUSTINE LOISEAU

The table is already set when we step inside the home of Patrick Bouju and Justine Loiseau in the hamlet of Glaine-Montaigut in the Auvergne. Featuring a simple white tablecloth, with polka-dotted navy blue plates and pristine Perceval steak knives made in nearby Thiers, the tablescape looks plucked from the pages of a magazine about French-country cooking.

 Beyond the table, the house is buzzing with the energy of a young family. Amidst scattered children's toys, Justine is putting the finishing touches on her slow-roasted lamb shank while handing us bountiful platters of vegetable side dishes to set on the table. Meanwhile, Patrick's animated musings on winemaking punctuate the air while he shuffles in and out of the house, trying to wrap up a few work obligations. Considering the couple manages Domaine la Bohème and two *négoce* projects—one on the Greek island of Samos and another operating on a large scale across France—while parenting two young children, it's surprising they've even found time to meet with us today, let alone cook. Yet it is precisely this unmistakable generosity that has helped establish them as influential mentors within the natural-wine movement.

 Born in Tours, Patrick first encountered natural wine while studying chemistry in Clermont-Ferrand in the 1990s. By that point, he had developed a general aversion to wine due to a severe intolerance to sulfites, which are prevalent in conventional wine. Then, in 1995, Patrick tasted a bottle that would change the course of his life: a sulfite-free white wine made by natural-wine trailblazer Thierry Puzelat in the Loire. A couple of years later, while looking for work, Patrick took over an abandoned parcel of vines and started making wine without sulfites as a hobby. Despite finding work as a computer engineer, he continued acquiring more vines and making wine on the side. In 2002, Patrick released his first commercial vintage, and by 2008, he had decided to quit his job to commit full-time to winemaking.

 Today, under the name Domaine La Bohème (a reference to Rimbaud's poem "Ma Bohème"), Patrick tends to eight hectares of vines.

WINERY

1. Patrick Bouju and Justine Loiseau share a moment in front of the hearth of their home in Glaine-Montaigut.

2. Perceval knives made in nearby Thiers have become an emblematic component of the natural-wine table, along with knives from Perceval alum, Roland Lannier.

3. Winemaker Patrick Bouju.

1

2

3

He produces an array of wines that adhere to zero-zero principles—meaning nothing is added or removed during the winemaking process, including sulfites. As a result, La Bohème cuvées vary year to year, but they never fail to hit a broad range of notes, from the fun and fruity, yet dry and deep, sparkling rosé Festejar! and the amphora-aged white blends like G&M to bigger reds like Cailloux, made from 120-year-old vines of gamay d'Auvergne and pinot noir.

By the time natural wine entered the broader cultural zeitgeist in the 2010s, Patrick's wines had already grabbed the attention of American rapper Action Bronson, who featured Patrick on an episode of his wildly popular VICE show *F*ck That's Delicious*. This encounter propelled Patrick into the limelight and led to the creation of À la Natural, a wine collaboration between Patrick, Action Bronson, and the multihyphenate French natural-wine rapper Clovis Ochin.

Patrick used his newfound worldwide notoriety to further promote zero-zero winemaking and develop two *négoce* projects. In 2018, after Justine joined him at the domaine, Patrick launched Sous le Végétal with pioneering Greek natural winemaker Jason Ligas from Domaine Ligas. Set on the Greek island of Samos, the project operates in partnership with a local cooperative of organic growers who believe in the importance of natural winemaking for the future.

In 2020, Patrick and Justine teamed up with fashion powerhouse couple Rosie and Max Assoulin to start Vivanterre, a large-scale *négoce* project that sources grapes across France. "We visit each winemaker and their vineyard to talk about their growing methods," says Justine, adding, "we'll never buy grapes grown with chemicals—the minimum requirement is that the winemaker must have been in organic conversion for at least one to two years." When harvest comes around, they take the grapes back to the Auvergne where they vinify them into five affordable cuvées labeled with straightforward names like White Petnat, Pink Petnat, White, Orange Contact, and Rouge Gamay.

With the domaine and both *négoce* projects combined, Patrick and Justine now produce an average of 100,000 bottles per year, a number made even more impressive knowing each grape is grown organically and vinified without sulfites. "Our idea is to democratize natural wine and show that it doesn't have to be a niche category,"

4

5

says Justine. "We are actually capable of producing large quantities without sulfites."

As a longtime advocate of zero-zero winemaking, Patrick has mentored several younger up-and-coming winemakers, such as Raphaël Beysang from Lapin des Vignes and Aurélien Lefort. Despite their strong beliefs, Patrick and Justine bring a "live and let live" attitude to the debate around the use of sulfites in natural wine. "Everyone is free to do whatever they want," says Patrick.

"It's a topic that is very divisive, and I think it's a shame," adds Justine. "We're faced with climate change, which impacts everything from viticulture to winemaking. It's more important that we pool our efforts to find answers to the problems we all face." Through Vivanterre, the couple has had the chance to meet numerous grape growers across France with whom they've discussed various climate change–induced struggles, from frost to droughts. "Whether you're in Alsace or Perpignan, we're all in the same boat," says Justine.

While Vivanterre and Sous le Végétal have helped the winemakers stay afloat during years when frost has destroyed most of Domaine la Bohème's production, it is evident that the ambition fueling both projects stretches far beyond the couple's own bottom line. By encouraging winemakers across two countries to convert to organic viticulture through thoughtful dialogue, Patrick and Justine aim to present a blueprint for the future of natural winemaking—one that operates at a much larger scale than the current norm.

"It's a bit of a crazy idea, and it's not easy, but we really have this ambition to show that this new model can be replicated," says Justine. "It's really about asking, how can we work together to change our current ways of doing things?"

WINERY   FR

4. Another empty bottle lineup, a sign of good times and good wine.

5. Sometimes old technology is the best technology.

6. A hearty piece of lamb that pulls apart with a gentle fork poke is the centerpiece of a cozy table.

6

BRAISED LAMB SHANK WITH SPELT

SERVES 6

"With two children and work, it's not always easy to prepare meals that are varied, balanced, and fun to eat," says Justine Loiseau. That explains why the winemaker favors set-and-forget dishes like this braised lamb shank, which spends over five hours in the oven, giving her time to play with her kids, help Patrick in the cellar, or entertain a group of visitors.

INGREDIENTS

Lamb Shank
- 1 lamb shank (about 3 ⅓ lbs)
- ½ cup extra-virgin olive oil
- Salt
- ½ tsp coriander seeds, crushed
- ½ tsp cumin seeds, crushed
- ½ tsp crushed Szechuan peppercorns
- 6 medium carrots, peeled and cut in half
- 5 small golden turnips, peeled and cut in half
- 3 small yellow onions, halved
- 3 cloves garlic, peeled and crushed
- 1 sprig rosemary
- 1 cup dry white wine

Spelt
- Salt
- 1 cup spelt berries, rinsed
- 4 tbs salted butter

INSTRUCTIONS

1. Preheat the oven to 350°F.

2. **For the lamb shank:** Coat the lamb shank with the olive oil and season with salt all over. Massage in with your hands. Sprinkle the crushed coriander, cumin, and Sichuan peppercorns all over and massage again.

3. In a large Dutch oven, add the seasoned lamb shank, carrots, turnips, onions, garlic, and rosemary sprig. Pour in 1 cup water and the white wine. Cover and transfer to the oven. Immediately lower the temperature to 230°F and gently braise until fork-tender, 4 to 5 hours, adding water or wine as needed to make sure there is always liquid at the bottom of the Dutch oven.

4. **For the spelt:** Bring a medium pot of salted water to a boil. Add the rinsed spelt berries and simmer, uncovered, until soft, 20 to 30 minutes. Drain the spelt and transfer to a serving bowl. Add the butter and toss until fully melted and combined.

5. Once the lamb is cooked, remove from the oven and serve immediately with the cooked spelt berries.

WINE BEETS AND CITRUS

SERVES 6

In places where wine flows like water, it's no surprise that everything is cooked in wine. While you can omit cooking the beets in wine, it does add another dimension to the earthy root vegetable. This dish is delicious served at room temperature, and alongside other salads, such as fennel, escarole, or celeriac.

INGREDIENTS

4 large beets
Salt
2 cloves
2 black peppercorns
4 **cups** dry red wine
1 **tsp** extra-virgin olive oil
Black pepper
½ **tsp** za'atar
Grated zest of 1 orange

INSTRUCTIONS

1. In a large pot, add the beets, 1 tsp salt, the cloves, peppercorns, red wine, and enough cold water to cover the beets. Bring to a boil, then lower the heat to medium and simmer until the beets are fork-tender, about 1 hour, depending on the size of your beets. Remove from the heat and let the beets cool down.

2. Once the beets are cool enough to handle, peel and cut them into bite-size pieces. Place them in a large bowl, then drizzle the beets with the olive oil and toss until they are fully coated. Finish with salt, pepper, za'atar, and orange zest.

Marie & Vincent Tricot

Tall, lean, and with a rugged handsomeness, Vincent Tricot moves through his vineyard, which is perched atop a verdant hill some twenty minutes outside Clermont-Ferrand, with the ease of someone who knows this land like the back of his hand. As he shows us around his newest plantings, a proud smile perks at the corners of his lips, where a twig from a vine dangles casually like a toothpick.

Vincent's winemaking journey originally stemmed from his passion for traveling. As a young man, Vincent yearned to see the world, and in order to fund his travels, he worked as a vine pruner near his parents' house in the Savennières vineyards. Eventually, he pursued studies in viticulture in the Beaujolais region, where he also worked part-time with the winemaking Cotton family. It was through this connection that he met Marie, who worked as a caregiver. The two fell in love, and, following Vincent's graduation, the couple packed their bags for Chile. Vincent found work with an industrial winery, while Marie dedicated her time to an orphanage.

After seven months in Chile and armed with invaluable experience, Vincent landed a job at a large winery in France, near Nîmes. The young winemaker longed to work for a domaine that crafted the types of wines he had grown to cherish during his time in Beaujolais, where he had the opportunity to interact with luminaries such as Marcel Lapierre, a trailblazer of the natural-wine movement. Since most smaller wineries couldn't afford to hire full-time help, Vincent made up his mind. "At one point, he declared, 'I'm sick and tired of having a boss. We've got to find our own spot,'" recalls Marie.

Strapped for cash but filled with optimism, they figured they could only afford land located in lesser-known winemaking regions. With this in mind, they visited Marie's family near Clermont-Ferrand in the Auvergne, a region with an all-but-forgotten winemaking history that is now primarily known for its scenic volcanic mountains and cheeses. "Back then, many people in France didn't even know that Auvergne wine existed," Marie explains.

During their visit, they learned of a domaine that was up for sale—five hectares of pristine vines that had been biodynamically farmed since the 1970s. "It was sheer luck," says Marie. "The owners were eager to breathe new life into the estate by passing it on to a young couple with children." About six months later,

1. Winemaker Vincent Tricot walking in his vineyard.

2. Driving around the Auvergne with Vincent.

with their two young daughters in tow, Marie and Vincent relocated to the Auvergne and started producing wine. Marie eventually left her job to focus on the sales aspect of the business, while Vincent immersed himself in tending to the vines and cellar.

Upon our return from the vineyard, we find Marie busy in the kitchen, enveloped in a cloud of savory aromas as she roasts a large hunk of lamb infused with generous amounts of garlic. If Vincent is known for his quiet confidence and measured way of speaking, Marie is his polar opposite. A goofball with a quick wit and a mischievous twinkle in her eye, she's not one to take herself too seriously. Leading us downstairs for the tasting portion of our visit, Marie opens a heavy wooden door to reveal the cellar. Inside, a dozen barrels, several amphoras, and a couple of fiberglass tanks line the walls, while fossilized spiders hang from the rafters. Vincent calmly guides us through the various cuvées, detailing each *cépage*, along with maceration times and temperatures. Meanwhile, Marie does her best to make us crack up with a few jokes. Naturally, we all let out a few boisterous laughs. With Marie's infectious joie de vivre balancing Vincent's monk-like dedication to the craft, it's easy to see why they form such a dynamic duo.

By the time Marie and Vincent started making wine in 2003, there were very few other natural winemakers in the region. This allowed them a lot of freedom to play around. Unlike more established regions like Burgundy, the Auvergne's identity had yet to be defined. And so, the plateaus and valleys became their playground on which to experiment and craft the kinds of wines they enjoyed drinking.

To honor their daughters, whose existence swayed the previous owners to sell them the land, Marie and Vincent repurposed their girls' drawings into labels for cuvées like Les Trois Bonhommes and Les Petites Fleurs. Adopting a gradual approach to sulfur-free winemaking, the couple steadily reduced additions year by year until 2011, when they ceased them altogether. The resulting red wines are devoid of any earthiness, instead boasting layers of dense, rich red fruit with soft tannins. The chardonnays exhibit notes of white mushrooms, a characteristic that is unique to the grape. They also craft delightful aromatic wines from newer plantings of sauvignon blanc and muscat.

Over the past few years, Auvergne wines have risen in popularity, thanks in part to the support of Parisian bistros like Le Verre Volé and Saturne. This surge has prompted more winemakers to follow in the footsteps of Vincent

2

3. (Left) Marie carves lamb for the table.
4. Marie and Vincent Tricot, through rosé-colored glasses.

and Marie. Beyond simply helping to establish a benchmark for Auvergne wines, the couple has succeeded in creating wines that reflect their own personalities: precise and measured like Vincent, light and vibrant like Marie.

Later that evening, after indulging in several bottles, and with all wine-related talk exhausted, Vincent puts on Zev's favorite Gainsbourg record. In a state of joyous inebriation, we burst into a dancing singalong. With the Auvergne's star on the rise, it would be understandable for the couple to feel a bit of pressure. But as the clock strikes 3 a.m, and Marie and Vincent's feet show no sign of slowing down, it's clear that no amount of international fascination could ever make those two lose their sense of play.

4

BAKING SHEET PEAR TART

MAKES 1 TART

Marie's simple pear tart recipe comes together super quickly, which means she can spend less time in the kitchen and more time with her friends. Plus, it makes for a delicious breakfast the next day when you're a bit too hungover to cook anything. Marie likes to make her tart with fruits grown by a friend who lives nearby and jam made by Vincent, using the apricots that grow on their land. To recreate this recipe at home, feel free to use store-bought apricot jam, or make your own by simmering 4 cups crushed apricots in a saucepan with 2½ cups sugar and 3 tbs fresh lemon juice until the mixture thickens.

INGREDIENTS

Dough
- 2½ **cups** all-purpose flour
- 1 **tsp** salt
- 2 **tsp** sugar
- ¾ **cup (1½ sticks)** unsalted butter, room temperature, cut into small cubes, plus additional for greasing

Pear Tart
- Flour, for dusting
- 4 **tbs** apricot jam
- 2 **lbs** ripe pears, thinly sliced lengthwise (Anjou, Bosc, or Bartlett)
- 4 **tbs (½ stick)** unsalted butter, cut into knobs
- 1 **tsp** sugar

INSTRUCTIONS

1. Preheat the oven to 350°F. Grease a large baking sheet with butter and set aside.

2. **For the dough:** In a large bowl, combine the flour, salt, sugar, and butter. Using your fingertips, blend the cubed butter into the flour until it starts to look like coarse sand. Gradually add in about 1 tbs water, and continue mixing until the ingredients come together. Knead until the dough looks smooth and feels elastic. Shape it into a disk, wrap it, and chill in the fridge for 15 minutes.

3. **For the tart:** On a lightly floured surface roll out the dough to the size of your baking sheet. Carefully transfer the dough to the prepared baking sheet and press it firmly against the edges. Trim any excess dough.

4. Spread the apricot jam on the dough. Arrange the pear slices on top with some overlap, scatter knobs of butter overtop, and sprinkle evenly with sugar. Transfer to the oven and bake until golden brown, about 30 minutes. Remove from the oven and allow the tart to cool down slightly before slicing and serving.

The Rhône

The Rhône Valley is named after the river that flows from the Swiss Alps, collecting snowmelt from the mountains on its way through Lake Geneva, before taking a sharp turn westward into southeastern France, and, finally, discharging its powerful stream into the Mediterranean Sea.

While the Rhône is mostly known for making big, powerful wines, reducing the winemaking culture of a region that stretches roughly 240 kilometers—from Vienne in the north to Avignon in the south—to just one style would be sacrilegious. (It would be like saying that the whole of the United States can be represented solely by the people of New York.) Every subregion of the Rhône carries its distinct culture along with a unique winemaking heritage.

In the northern reaches, where the staggeringly steep hills of Cornas, Côte-Rôtie, and Hermitage flank the river, syrah predominantly flourishes in the region's granite and schist soils. These grapes are mostly vinified into deep red wines with grippy tannins and a telltale black-pepper spice. Starting in the 1980s, trailblazing winemakers René-Jean Dard and François Ribo were among the first to go against the grain and produce additive-free syrah in the northern Rhône.

As you journey downstream into Ardèche, where the array of soils is matched only by the variety of cépages, a realm of possibilities unfolds. Here, grapes like grenache, merlot, cabernet sauvignon, gamay, pinot noir, cinsault, and carignan team up with syrah to craft a diverse array of wines. White-wine production within this subregion, on the other hand, is dominated by chardonnay and viognier. The broader natural-wine revolution in the Rhône region found its origins in southern Ardèche, thanks to Gérald Oustric of Le Mazel and his accomplice Gilles Azzoni from Le Raisin et L'Ange. Steadfast in their quest to mentor and turn young winemakers onto zero-zero winemaking, they have dedicated decades to sharing their grapes and land with anyone ready to embrace the movement. Today, cascading down the hill from Le Mazel, you'll find several dozen small producers releasing exceptional natural wines. These wines span from reds with robust tannins typical of the region to fresh carbonic reds, *pét-nats*, and luscious white wines.

As you continue your journey south toward the western stretches of the Rhône, you'll arrive in the Gard, near the town of Uzès. In this locale, a band of misfits, weary of urban life, has congregated to farm the land under the Mediterranean sun. In recent years, microwineries have emerged overnight in unexpected places, such as garages and abandoned co-ops. Collectively they form one of the most compelling clusters of the country's natural-wine movement, challenging the long-standing notion that the Rhône is synonymous with robust, tannic, and potent wines. Following in the footsteps of Eric Pfifferling from Domaine de L'Anglore, the kids of Uzès are pressing vibrant and acidity-driven translucent red wines that not only mirror the enthusiasm of the movement but also elevate it.

Beyond the well-documented famous appellations, many aspiring vignerons with limited resources have found their niche in lesser-known corners of the Rhône. Here, ancient vines and unique microclimates abound. Thanks to fermentation techniques passed down from previous generations, there's an opportunity to blend the region's sun-soaked fruit with gentler macerations and fermentations. The result? Fresh, approachable wines that carry the memory of their sunny growing season, kissed by candy-like fruit.

In the following pages, you will become acquainted with winemakers who exemplify various facets of the wine culture in Ardèche and the Gard. The Rhône-born duo behind Les Deux Terres showed us what it means to celebrate their Ardéchois roots with vibrant country wines and one hyper-regional dish. Meanwhile, transplants like former Noma sommelier Anders Frederik Steen and Parisian party-girl-turned-winemaker Lolita Sene, have garnered international recognition for their lively wines and unique labels and stayed true to themselves with dishes that reflect their individual cultural backgrounds.

1. Anne Brunn Blauert on a hike in Valvignères, looking over the valley, which the Romans called Vallis Vinaria (the valley of vines).

Lolita Sene

It's getting late, but Xavier remains determined to see this game of backgammon through. Like clockwork, we stretch our legs, pour ourselves a glass of Papanapator, light another cigarette, and settle back into our cross-legged positions around winemaker Lolita Sene's coffee table. In the corner of the hazy living room, Lolita smiles tenderly as she shares a moment with her partner, Nicolas Renaud, the winemaker behind Le Clos des Grillons. Tonight marks the couple's first evening alone since the birth of their daughter a few months prior. Glancing over at the lovebirds illuminated only by the flickering glow of the fireplace, Steph smirks. "I think it's time for us to go," she whispers.

While motherhood has ushered in a series of new beginnings for Lolita, it isn't the first time the young winemaker has reinvented herself, which might explain why she is so hard to pin down. Sure, Lolita could easily be described as intelligent, beautiful, and free-spirited. But perhaps the most fitting shorthand is to say that she is a "Jessa"—the whimsical, uncontainable character portrayed by Jemima Kirke in HBO's *Girls*, a show that so aptly captured and defined the millennial generation. Much like Jessa, Lolita exudes an air of it-girl confidence and impenetrability that casts a spell on whoever she meets.

Born in Montpellier in 1987, Lolita grew up as an artsy child who excelled academically. She remained relatively quiet until her late teens, when she moved to Paris to pursue a career in advertising. She later transitioned into working as a club promoter, but by the time she managed to open her own nightclub on rue de Rivoli in Paris, her party-girl habits had caught up with her. She was hooked on cocaine and out of control. (Lolita chronicled her tumultuous struggle with addiction and subsequent overdose in *C., La face noire de la blanche*, a critically acclaimed autobiographical novel she penned after getting sober.)

"After achieving sobriety, I realized that the nightlife scene wasn't where I wanted to spend the rest of my life," Lolita reflects. With uncertainty looming over her next steps, she turned to Google and stumbled upon winemaking—a field that promised to blend her passion for science, creativity, and social interaction. She enrolled in an agronomy program in Montpellier and supported herself by working at a restaurant, where she met a sommelier who introduced her to natural wine.

"The conventional wines we studied in school left me uninspired," recalls Lolita. "But natural wine was a revelation. It was different, punk, fun, and cool. It gave me goosebumps."

Lolita pursued a master's degree in business in Paris, while picking up freelance writing gigs and further immersing herself in the world of wine by working at a wine shop. When an opportunity arose in 2016 to work as a sommelier in Canada while writing travel guides for a French website, she eagerly seized it. The experience cemented her love affair with wine.

Two years later, Lolita returned to France with the intention of making wine. To her surprise, opportunities came knocking sooner than expected, and she was offered grapes to purchase as well as a shared winery space. "Everything happened so quickly; it felt like speeding down a freeway," Lolita recalls. "I didn't know how to do anything."

Despite her formal winemaking training, Lolita did was most people of her generation do when they find themselves stumped: she watched a lot of YouTube tutorials. With the added guidance of her winemaker friends, her first year yielded 1,500 bottles. Shortly after harvest, the budding winemaker purchased her first piece of land—a small plot of grenache near the picturesque town of Uzès—solidifying her commitment to winemaking.

Five vintages later, Lolita now owns just over one hectare of land divided into four parcels

1

where she grows grenache, syrah, and cinsault grapes that she vinifies separately. (She plans to introduce muscat in the future.) To supplement her production, she also sources grapes from local growers, accounting for roughly 40 percent of her total grape supply.

Lolita combines her minimalistic approach to winemaking with playful labels and cuvée names (Papanapator is a phonetic interpretation of the French "daddy's always right") to craft wines that very much feel like her. "Precise but impatient, you know?" she muses. "For instance, this year I'm releasing all my wines *en primeur*, because I just wanted to get them out there right away." Lolita's wines embody the essence of spontaneity: perfect for tossing in your tote bag for an impromptu park hang with your crush or a leisurely day lounging by the pool (especially if your bikini matches the leopard print one featured on the label of her Tralala cuvée).

With a flourishing wine business, a partner, a child, and a house, does the thirty-something feel settled? Not quite. After all, she's a Jessa. "My biggest dream would be to make a living from writing," she shares. "And then? You know, when I'm sixty or something, I'd love to open a cinema or a theater." At the time of writing this book, Lolita has just released her second novel, *Un été chez Jida*, which draws inspiration from her Kabyle heritage (don't miss her grandmother's recipe for couscous with lamb on p.146). Rest assured, however, that no matter what chapter comes next in the book of Lolita's life, she promises to always make wine, even if it's just a single cuvée. "When you fall so deeply in love with winemaking," she says, "it's hard to get out."

1. Winemaker Lolita Sene in her winery.
2. Lolita gathers the ingredients to prepare her family's Kabyle Couscous with Lamb.
3. A heated game of backgammon in Lolita's living room.
4. Science.

KABYLE COUSCOUS WITH LAMB

SERVES 6–8

Although born in Paris, Lolita Sene is of multiple ethnicities—she is French on her father's side and Kabyle, a Berber ethnic group, on her mother's side. From the mountains of Algeria, her mother's family trekked to France, living in several camps along the way, before settling in Marseille. This lamb and couscous recipe, which is portioned to feed a large family or dinner party, has been passed down through generations of Lolita's family. According to Lolita, the slow, traditional process of preparing couscous allows her to reflect on her family's difficult past while tapping into joyful memories of time spent in the kitchen with her elders.

INGREDIENTS

Lamb
4 lbs lamb neck and shoulder chops, cut into 1-inch chunks
Salt
4 tbs extra-virgin olive oil
1 medium yellow onion, peeled and quartered
2 tbs ground cumin
2 tbs sweet paprika
1 tbs tomato paste
1 tsp harissa paste
1 cup roughly chopped carrots
1 cup roughly chopped zucchini
1 cup turnip wedges
1 cup roughly chopped celery
1 cup cleaned and roughly chopped leeks
1 (15.5-oz) can chickpeas

Couscous
2 lbs couscous
1 tsp salt
2 tbs extra-virgin olive oil

INSTRUCTIONS

1. **For the lamb:** Pat the lamb dry with a paper towel. Season generously with salt. In a large Dutch oven, heat the olive oil over medium-high heat. Add the lamb and sear until golden, about 2 minutes each side.

2. Add the onion and cook until fragrant and beginning to soften, about 5 minutes. Stir in the cumin, paprika, tomato paste, and harissa. Add 1 cup of water and bring to a boil. Add the carrots, zucchini, turnips, and celery. Add more water until the pot is about three quarters full. Bring to a simmer over medium-high heat, then reduce the heat to low and cook until the lamb pieces are tender, about 1 hour. Add the leeks and chickpeas to the Dutch oven. Reduce the heat to low and simmer for 2 hours, until fork-tender.

3. **For the couscous:** In a large bowl, add the couscous, salt, and olive oil, tossing to coat. Add ¼ cup water and mix using your hands to allow the couscous to slowly absorb the water (the motion should feel like you are mixing dough to make bread). Continue adding water slowly and stirring with your hands. Once you have added about 2 cups of water, cover the couscous with a cloth and let it rest for 30 minutes. Once the couscous has rested, continue adding water, slowly, while mixing with your hands, up to 2 additional cups. Taste it as you go. (You want the couscous to be soft but not too wet, so you may not need to add all the water.)

4. Divide the couscous into bowls and top with the lamb and vegetable stew. Serve immediately.

Anders Frederik Steen & Anne Bruun Blauert

The sun is pounding just about as hard as Steph's headache as she wanders the streets of Valvignères looking for a place, any place, that would be open for coffee during the middle of the day. The previous night's festivities at La Tour Cassée, a legendary locale for natural-wine lovers in Ardèche, have finally caught up with her. While the hotel is no longer in operation, La Tour Cassée's owner, Claire Bouveron, graciously agreed to accommodate a few travelers in town for the wine fair. As those things tend to go, dozens of winemakers, importers, and restaurateurs descended on the hotel to eat, drink, and play pool until the wee hours of the morning. Hence, the raging headache and quest for caffeine.

Just when she was about to give up and resort herself to curling up into a ball somewhere in an alley, Steph hears a familiar voice: "Need help?" shouts winemaker Anders Frederik Steen from across the street. Tired but decidedly less hungover than her, the winemaker graciously invites Steph in and offers to make coffee for the both of them.

With its rustic French bones dressed in garbs of minimalist Danish furniture and art, Anders's house looks straight out of an interior-design magazine. As she walks inside, where less than twenty-four hours ago, bright-eyed and bushy tailed, she enjoyed a wholesome lunch the Anders, his wife, Anne Bruun Blauert, and their daughter, Ingeborg, Steph notices Anders's book, *Poetry Is Growing in our Garden*, proudly propped on the kitchen island.

A collection of thoughts and observations on life and winemaking, the book is a

2

3

1. (Left) Winemaker Anne Brunn Blauert in her kitchen in Valvignère, where Scandinavian simplicity meets French countryside richness.

2. Winemaker Anders Frederik Steen.

3. Located in the heart of Valvignère, the restaurant and hotel La Tour Cassée is a natural-wine institution in Ardèche—some people (Zev) have even labeled it "The Best Hotel in the World."

4. Anders and Anne's daughter Ingebord, following in her father's footsteps, starts her sommelier training early by opening a bottle of wine for us to enjoy over lunch.

5. La Tour Cassée owner, Claire Bouveron, ever diligent, keeps order.

reflection of Anders's mind: dense, poetic, and highly contemplative. As its title suggests, *Poetry Is Growing in our Garden* is about noticing the beauty in the everyday and turning the mundane into something greater than the sum of its parts—a quest that has guided Anders throughout his life.

Anders was raised in a multifamily home on the outskirts of Copenhagen, which he describes as a kind of spiritual second-cousin to the hippie communes of the 1960s. Fascinated by people, he enrolled in psychology in college. In order to pay the bills, Anders worked in kitchens. The hospitality industry quickly turned into a passion against which psychology didn't stand a chance.

At the time, molecular gastronomy was all the rage. For a lot of young cooks hoping to stand out, the best move was to land a stage with the master himself, Ferran Adrià, at El Bulli in Spain. Instead of following in his cohorts' footsteps, Anders chose to expand his culinary knowledge through wine education. He landed a job as a sommelier at a new Copenhagen restaurant by the name of Noma. (Anders would later go on to help open Manfreds and Relæ.) On his days off, the young sommelier would travel to London to complete his WSET wine-training course.

Anders also took frequent trips to Paris to explore the city's blossoming natural-wine scene. There, he befriended a slew of winemakers, including Gérald Oustric from domaine Le Mazel, Gilles Azzoni from Le Raisin et L'Ange, and the legendary Jura vigneron, Jean-Marc

Brignot. Soon, Anders began importing some of his favorite discoveries back to Copenhagen. Around the same time, Anders and Anne, who had met while working at an amusement park in their early twenties, got married and had two children, Verner and Ingeborg.

In 2013, at the behest of his friend Gilles Azzoni in Ardèche, Anders decided to try his hand at making wine with the help of Jean-Marc Brignot. Meanwhile, Anne continued building her career as a social worker in prisons around Copenhagen.

After spending a few harvest seasons apart, the family uprooted from Denmark in 2016 to focus on Anders's wine project (Jean-Marc had moved to Japan). Anne saw this as an opportunity for a more balanced family life. "We could live differently as a family and still do something that is meaningful and fun, instead of coming home late at night with a headache because of problems at work," she explains.

With no wine background, Anne brought a fresh perspective to the operation. While most people in the wine world are often afraid to ask questions for fear of sounding stupid, Anne was fearless. Her curiosity led to questioning and exploring new approaches. "When Anne came in, our wines became more relaxed and focused," says Anders. "We started making the wine we'd always wanted."

Steen wines are widely known for their evocative labels that feature single-line quotes derived from a story or something overheard on the street like Wear Me Like a Flower, Bad Lighting Call You Later, and The Sound of People Clapping Improves When It's Raining. Yet, Anders is wary of assigning figurative labels to his wines. "I think you should see them more as postcards from a vacation, a temporary snapshot of what is going on in two people's lives in a certain moment," he says. Anne, the more pragmatic of the two, interjects. "Don't you think that they have a certain style? If you were to talk to someone who's never had the wines, you wouldn't say 'this is a piece of my family history,'" she says, laughing. "That's true," agrees Anders, joining in his wife's laughter.

Describing Steen wines is a daunting task. Behind each individual label is a wine that has been treated as such. As a disciple of Brignot and Bruno Schueller, Anders believes in allowing wines the time they need. Made with grapes from both Ardèche and Alsace, the wines range from youthful, fruity rosé pét-nats to deep, oxidative Alsatian field blends aged for five years in barrel. By design, this diversity ensures Steen wines resist categorization, inviting reinterpretation over time—much like their labels.

The significance of those labels became apparent to Anders in 2015 when he received a message from a Brazilian woman seeking bottles of a wine from his first vintage, Sweet Beginning of a Better End. She explained that a few months earlier, during the finalization of her divorce, she and her husband embarked on one last trip together to California. One evening, a server at a wine bar recommended Sweet Beginning of a Better End, a name too serendipitous for a couple undergoing a divorce to forget.

As the contents of the bottle dwindled throughout the night, the couple found themselves falling back in love with each other. And now, the woman was looking for more bottles to serve at their vow-renewal ceremony. "We write short sentences on the labels that explain our relationship to the wine," says Anders. "But when other people read the name of the cuvée, they start to think of something else because they have another history, other experiences. So for them the title means something else. That I find very beautiful."

In many ways, Anders, as a winemaker, is a lot like a poet. Granted, if you understand winemaking and poetry in a very conventional way, one as a chemical process and the other as the art of crafting beautiful words into prose, they bear almost no resemblance. But if you see poetry as enhancing something that is already beautiful, then it becomes closely intertwined with winemaking. "Poetry is noticing small, beautiful things and putting them together to create something extraordinary that brings about imagination and feelings," explains Anders. The act of picking grapes and fermenting them into wine is a winemaker's sonnet, a creation open to myriad interpretations depending on the person it touches. "I think poetry and winemaking are similar because people actually receive more than what you give."

WILD MUSHROOM RISOTTO

SERVES 4–6

Arriving in Valvignères after a week of indulging in hearty braised meat dishes, we were desperate for vegetables. Anders and Anne's kitchen island, overflowing with greens, was a sight for sore eyes. It felt as though they had read our minds. We savored fresh radishes dipped in cultured butter as we observed Anders preparing his version of mushroom risotto. While some treat mushrooms as merely a garnish, the winemaker prefers to roast them first, infusing them into the risotto's stock for added earthiness and depth.

INGREDIENTS

- 4 cloves garlic
- 3 **tbs** extra-virgin olive oil
- 1 sprig thyme
- 1 **tsp** fresh rosemary leaves
- 1 **cup** seasonal wild mushrooms, cleaned and chopped (we like chanterelles and morels)
- 2 **cups** dry white wine
- 2 **cups** chicken stock or vegetable broth
- 2 small onions, finely chopped
- 2½ **cups** Arborio rice
- Salt and black pepper
- Grated zest of 1 lemon
- ¼ **cup** freshly grated Parmigiano Reggiano

INSTRUCTIONS

1. Crush 2 garlic cloves and finely chop the remaining 2 cloves. Pour 1 tbs olive oil into a medium pot on medium heat, add the crushed garlic, and cook until they take on some color, about 1 minute. Add the thyme, rosemary, and wild mushrooms and continue cooking until the mushrooms take on some color, 2 to 3 minutes. Add the white wine and reduce completely. Add the stock and reduce by half. Set aside to cool.

2. In a large skillet set over low heat, add 1 tbs olive oil, the finely chopped garlic, and the onions. Sweat for a few minutes, making sure the onions don't take on any color. Add the rice and toast, stirring to prevent burning, until the rice becomes glossy, about 2 minutes. Add just enough stock from the pot with the mushrooms to cover the rice, and stir just once to prevent sticking or burning. When most of the stock has reduced, add a little more stock. Repeat this process until all the stock has been added and the rice is tender but not mushy. You can add more water if the rice is still crunchy after you use up all the stock.

3. Add the mushrooms to the rice and season with salt and pepper. Add the lemon zest, the remaining 1 tbs olive oil, and grated Parmigiano Reggiano. Stir to combine. Let the risotto sit for 5 minutes. Taste and adjust the seasoning with salt and pepper. Serve immediately.

BROCCOLINI WITH PRESERVED LEMONS

SERVES 4

For this simple side dish, Anders uses small, slender broccolini harvested from Anne's spring garden. "They offer a more delicate flavor profile, less akin to cabbage and more reminiscent of asparagus," remarks the winemaker.

INGREDIENTS

- 1 lb broccolini
- Salt
- ½ tsp black pepper
- Grated zest and juice of 1 lemon
- 1 preserved lemon (store-bought or homemade)
- 2 to 3 tbs extra-virgin olive oil

INSTRUCTIONS

1. Bring a large pot of salted water to a boil. Meanwhile, prepare a large bowl of ice water. Add the broccolini to the pot of boiling water and blanch until just tender, but not soft, about 3 minutes. Using tongs, remove the Broccolini from the water and immediately plunge them in the bowl of ice water to stop them from cooking further.

2. Drain the broccolini, then arrange on a platter and drizzle with lemon juice and olive oil. Finish with ½ tsp salt, the pepper, lemon zest, oil from the preserved lemons, and some preserved lemon zest. Serve immediately.

Les Deux Terres

VINCENT FARGIER & MANU CUNIN

"I could watch them do pretty much anything without ever getting bored," says Steph, pointing at Vincent Fargier and Manu Cunin in the kitchen. From the dining table where we are sitting, it's hard to tell if the men behind Les Deux Terres are more interested in roasting each other or the *caillettes* (p.160) they've prepared for us, using meat from a pig Vincent butchered with his father the previous week. Vincent, with his broad smile, towers a good foot above Manu's dark, unruly hair, making the duo look like the French countryside's answer to Arnold Schwarzenegger and Danny DeVito in the 1988 comedy *Twins*. But when two people work together for a long time like these two have, they start to sound more like an old couple than long-lost brothers, effortlessly finishing each other's sentences and anticipating the other's needs. In many ways, the story of Vincent's and Manu's winemaking partnership reads more like a love story than a buddy comedy—meet-cute, family drama, and happy ending included.

While they were both born in Ardèche where they now make wine, Manu and Vincent come from fairly different cultural backgrounds. Vincent grew up heir apparent to his father's six hectares of vines situated just outside Villeneuve de Berg, a small village edging toward the mountains. Like two generations of men before him, he was set to farm the land and sell his grapes to the local cooperative that would turn them into the region's trademark tannic, grippy red wines.

Meanwhile, Manu's childhood was divorced from the land, his parents having chosen to ditch their ancestors' agricultural backgrounds in favor of more regular jobs. Vincent went to agricultural school to follow in his father's footsteps, while Manu moved to Montpellier to work in the music industry. After growing tired from

1. "Twins" Vincent Fargier and Manu Cunin bicker about salting the caillettes.

2. Winemaker Manu Cunin.

3. Winemaker Vincent Fargier.

the industry's party lifestyle and with a newborn in tow, Manu decided to move back to Ardèche and give agriculture a shot. He enrolled in the local agricultural college where Vincent, who was in his early twenties, was teaching. "There was a spark between us," says Manu, talking about the immediate connection he felt with Vincent when they first met.

Around the same time, the pair started hanging out with Gérald Oustric from Domaine Le Mazel and Gilles Azzoni from Le Raisin et L'Ange, the godfathers of Ardèche's natural-wine movement. With the guidance of Oustric and Azzoni, who were proponents of zero-zero winemaking, Vincent and Manu quickly started dreaming of their own project. However, they had to do so in secret because Vincent's dad would not have approved of taking the family's vines out of the local cooperative. While some winemakers who work without sulfur or any other additives take a very laissez-faire approach to winemaking, accepting that their wines might develop faulty characteristics, Manu and Vincent were never fond of such twists and turns. From the beginning, the pair wanted to take a very precise approach to produce highly drinkable wines that represented Ardèche and the Northern Rhône.

Around the time Vincent's father retired in 2008, Manu purchased his own parcel of vines. "Vincent already had six hectares of land from his father, and when I finally found my parcels, we thought it would be interesting to combine both terroirs," says Manu. And so, Les Deux Terres (The Two Lands) was born.

In 2010, eager to promote the growing natural-wine movement they'd helped create in Ardèche, Oustric and Azzoni took Vincent and Manu to the Loire's premier natural-wine fairs, La Dive and La Remise, to showcase their first vintage. Les Deux Terres was an instant success. "We sold thirteen thousand bottles during those two fairs," says Manu. "Vincent's father was finally reassured."

When we reach Manu over the phone a year after our visit, the winemaker is recovering from an injury that prevented him from working harvest. The time off, it seems, has allowed him to reflect on the past and the future of Les Deux Terres. "I can't talk about our wines without thinking about Vincent," says Manu. "Whenever Gilles Azzoni tastes our wines, he tries to guess who made each one. And most of the time he fails because when Vincent and I work together, we become one entity."

Talking to Manu about Vincent feels like getting a relationship master class. "We always said we didn't know if this would last. Now we're like an old couple, we've been doing this for thirteen years," he says. All those years since their meet-cute at the agricultural college, Manu and Vincent, who enjoy separate lives outside of work with different groups of friends, still find ways to reignite the spark that brought them together in the first place. "Recently we attended Les 10 Vins Cochons wine fair. It had been a while since we had done that because we don't really need to go to fairs to sell wine anymore. But we had so much fun. It felt like we were kids all over again." Another key to the success of their partnership is a rule they instated at the very beginning. "We said to each other, laughing, that whoever speaks the loudest makes the decision. And once a decision has been made, we never look back and say we should have done it differently," says Manu. "We don't want to always be thinking about what could've been. We want to move forward."

When talking about wine, people often say that a bottle is a snapshot of a specific place at a specific moment in time. Manu's and Vincent's wines feel like so much more than that. Each bottle from Les Deux Terres is a snapshot of a friendship between two wildly different people who found each other serendipitously, and now create something special. "We always said that if one of us wanted to stop, Les Deux Terres would cease to exist. Maybe we'd continue making wine separately, but nobody would take over the domaine. It will forever be an adventure that we went on together, just the two of us."

5

4

4-5. A big trend we noticed during our travels: natural-wine-themed books and cartoons were on full display in most French winemakers' bathrooms.

6. (Right) Manu takes the caillettes and potato pancakes out of the oven while Vincent takes stock.

CAILLETTES

SERVES 6–8

In Ardèche, pig farming is deeply rooted in culinary and cultural traditions. La Fête du Cochon, (Pig Festival), held in the winter months, marks the end of the pig-raising season. Families gather to butcher the pig and transform all its parts into various products like sausages, hams, terrines, boudin noir, and caillettes—small pork patties wrapped in caul fat (a net-like membrane that surrounds the pig's organs), and incorporating blanched cabbage or Swiss chard leaves for added flavor. When we visited Les Deux Terres in February 2022, we had missed the festival by a week or so, but the caillettes Vincent prepared for us were made with the pig he had butchered with his father for the festivities. If you can't find caul fat at your local butcher, you can wrap the caillettes in blanched chard leaves.

INGREDIENTS

Special equipment: Meat grinder (optional)

Salt
16 medium leaves of Swiss chard, stems removed
1 lb fresh boneless pork loin
½ lb bacon
½ lb pork liver (or a combination of heart, kidneys, and spleen)
1 clove garlic
1 tsp fresh thyme
1 tsp black pepper
Enough unsalted butter to grease the inside of a large baking dish
3–4 pieces caul fat (each about 10 inches square)

INSTRUCTIONS

1. Preheat the oven to 400°F.

2. Bring a medium pot of salted water to a boil. Add the chard and blanch until wilted but not mushy, about 2 minutes. Squeeze the chard to drain it and then chop it roughly.

3. If you are using a meat grinder, roughly cut the pork loin, bacon, and liver into small cubes. Add them to the meat grinder along with the chard leaves and garlic, making sure the grind is not too fine. If you don't have a meat grinder, cut the meat into ¼-inch pieces, mince the garlic, and finely chop the chard.

4. Combine in a large bowl and add the thyme, 1 tbs salt, and the pepper. Working with your hands, mix until the meat is combined with all the ingredients. Divide the meat into 12 to 16 balls the size of a clementine. Set aside.

5. Grease a large baking dish with butter and set aside. In a medium bowl, soak the caul fat for 5 minutes in cold salted water, then rinse and squeeze to drain. Cut it into 5-inch squares.

6. Wrap each meatball in caul fat. Space the caillettes evenly in the greased baking dish and bake about 45 minutes, until golden brown on top. Serve immediately.

The Languedoc

With vines as far as the eye can see, the Languedoc can be a disorienting experience. France's largest and highest-producing wine region spanning a variety of landscapes, the Languedoc runs from the Mediterranean coastline to the foothills of the Pyrenees Mountains and the Massif Central. But as the saying goes, more isn't always better. In the case of the Languedoc, where the production of high volumes of wine has supplanted quality, this definitely holds true.

It's no coincidence that so much wine comes out of the Languedoc, as the region benefits from an array of elements that make it a winemaker's dream. Large, flat valleys surrounded by steep hills thick with garigue, the region's mixed and aromatic shrubbery, make tractor farming a breeze. The region's Mediterranean climate provides ample sunshine throughout the growing season, which promotes grape ripening. Moderate rainfalls help grape development, while the generally dry climate reduces the risk of fungal diseases that can harm grapevines.

The soil varies significantly throughout the region, from limestone and clay in some areas to schist and gravel in others. This contributes unique characteristics to the wines, allowing for the cultivation of various grape varieties and the production of a wide range of wine styles. (Clay, in particular, is great at retaining water, which helps during extremely hot and dry summers.)

The Languedoc boasts a long, rollercoaster-like history of winemaking that dates back to Roman times, when its wines were sought throughout the empire. However, the region's prosperity took a hit in the thirteenth century during the Albigensian Crusade, when its vineyards became battlegrounds. Despite this setback, the region recovered and flourished again. Starting in the nineteenth century, the growing demand for inexpensive table wine, along with the opportunity to generate profit, encouraged Languedoc winemakers to turn to mass production. Near the end of the nineteenth century, the devastation caused by the phylloxera epidemic led to the replanting of hardy, high-yielding grape varieties, leading to a loss of diversity. Throughout the twentieth century, technological advancements and improved transportation networks further solidified the region's reputation for quantity over quality.

Luckily, there is a silver lining to all of this. The Languedoc's bargain reputation, combined with the absence of a comprehensive appellation system, has kept land prices relatively low compared to its neighbors to the north. This has helped transform the region into a hotbed for natural winemakers looking to produce higher-quality, terroir-driven wines farmed without systemic chemicals. Plus, the region's trademark garigue fosters a balanced ecosystem, thick with yeast complexes, that is prime for jump-starting fermentations naturally.

While grenache and syrah continue to reign supreme, along with large-scale winery favorites cabernet sauvignon and merlot, natural winemakers have embraced a variety of compelling, lesser-known grapes like cinsault, terret, grenache gris and blanc, chenin, mauzac, and various muscats. Additionally, the natural-wine movement has introduced skin macerations, *pét-nats*, and lighter red wines to a region typically known for producing tannic, rich reds and oily white wines.

In the following pages, we will introduce you to the king and queen of the South, Jean-Baptiste and Charlotte Sénat, whose tireless commitment to community building has helped elevate the Languedoc's natural-wine scene. The recipe we selected from Charlotte's impressive repertoire reflects not only the winemaker's natural disposition but also mirrors her region: sunny and generous.

Charlotte & Jean-Baptiste Sénat

Moments before we pull into Jean-Baptiste and Charlotte Sénat's driveway in the small commune of Trausse, in the Minervois, our phones buzz with a text from Charlotte. In less than twenty-four hours, the couple is set to host Le Vin de Mes Amis, one of the largest natural-wine fairs in the South of France. But as the text reveals, Charlotte will now have to manage it alone: Jean-Baptiste (J-B for short) has just been admitted to the hospital.

Despite her husband being in the hospital, a long list of last-minute tasks for the fair, and having to give us a full tour of the vineyards before cooking dinner, Charlotte remains not only unflappable but also unbelievably warm and charming. When she greets us, draped in a royal purple bouclé jacket and sporting a bold, red lip framed by an impeccable blowout, the winemaker reassures us there is nothing to worry about, J-B is doing fine. "Alors, vous êtes prêts?" she asks, ready to take us on a walk around the domaine and vineyard.

Owned by Jean-Baptiste's family for generations, the domaine is nestled within a u-shaped multifamily home the couple shares with other relatives. The stone building, weathered by time and bathed in sunlight, is adorned with vibrant red doors, windows, and wrought iron gates, and lush green vines cascading up the walls. Behind the house lies a prolific garden where the air is filled with the fragrant aromas of wild herbs and flowers. Welcome to the South of France!

Charlotte and J-B are affectionately known as the queen and king of the South, a title they've earned through their unwavering dedication to southern terroir and the community they've built around it for over twenty-five years. It's the kind of longevity neither of them anticipated when their journey began.

Both raised in Paris, Charlotte initially pursued law studies while Jean-Baptiste majored in history and political science. In 1995, disillusioned after a few unhappy years in politics, Jean-Baptiste convinced Charlotte to relocate to his family domaine in the Minervois, where they would start making wine. He hired a seasoned winemaker to teach him the craft and immersed himself in the writings of Jules Chauvet. A series of encounters with generous artisan winemakers eventually steered him toward organic viticulture and natural winemaking.

1

2

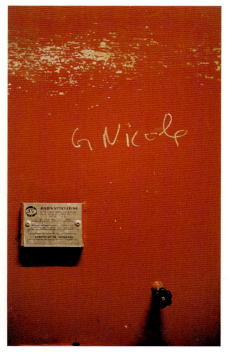

1. Winemaker Charlotte Sénat.

2. Epoxy-lined steel tank filled with wine waiting for bottling.

3. French people call pinball "flipper."

At the time, natural wine was virtually unheard of in the region. Seeking to break their isolation, the couple started attending some of France's first natural-wine fairs, like La Dive Bouteille, where they connected with like-minded winemakers such as Philippe and Cécile Valette (p.114), who would become lifelong friends. Still disheartened by the absence of natural-wine fairs in the south, Charlotte and Jean-Baptiste decided to take matters into their own hands and organize their own.

"We realized early on that the more of us there were, the stronger this movement would become," says Charlotte. The first edition of Le Vin de Mes Amis was held in Montpellier in 2004 and featured twenty-seven winemakers. More than twenty years later, the couple now hosts two editions of the fair each year, one in Montpellier and another in Paris, showcasing over 100 producers.

3

The following morning, we rendezvous with Charlotte at the impressive Domaine de Verchant in Castelnau-le-Lez, Montpellier. The morning sunlight is streaming into the castle's courtyard, casting a golden glow over the already bustling scene of Le Vin de Mes Amis. We make our rounds, stopping at various tables to taste and chat with a variety of winemakers, ranging from veterans like Jean Foillard to up-and-comers like Lolita Sene (p.142). In the heart of the main room, we observe Charlotte holding court with natural ease and glamour.

To pass the time before the legendary dinner of Le Vin de Mes Amis, an event that brings together winemakers and fair attendees for a gastronomic extravaganza, we opt to explore some of the smaller natural-wine fairs taking place in Montpellier that day. In stark contrast to the grandeur of Le Vin de Mes Amis, these smaller fairs have more of a DIY approach. Instead of a castle, fairs like Les Vignerons de L'Irréel host a surprising number of new producers, many of whom are presenting their first or second vintages inside a community sports center.

"Young people today move so much faster than we did. There are so many tastings, wine bars, and winemakers, and so, young winemakers who are starting out know exactly what kind of wine they want to make right away," says a fully-recovered Jean-Baptiste when we speak to him a few months after our visit. "They have more tools. I just don't know if they'll accept the slowness of the business in the same way," adds Charlotte, referring to the slow pace that's inherent to winemaking.

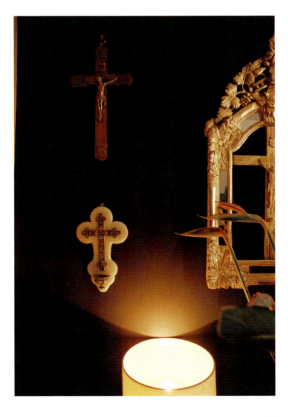

When they set up shop over twenty-five years ago, Jean-Baptiste and Charlotte thought their winemaking experiment would last at most ten years. Each vintage presented a new opportunity to try something new, which was exciting, but then they had to wait another year to apply their learnings and push their experiments further. The couple quickly realized that investing in their craft and environment, with new plantings and vineyard experimentation, would require a serious commitment on their part. "A lot of young people today are either buying grapes or juice from different places. They're less attached to a single region, whereas we continue to be fully anchored in our terroir," says J-B.

They may not be the most tagged winery on Instagram, but for the queen and king of the South, that's beside the point. "It's about making wines that we like, that are appreciated by people, while maintaining our identity instead of following trends," says Charlotte. "We're not in the Jura, we're not in Beaujolais, we're in the South. So we still have to make wines that retain our southern identity."

Other markers of success they consider, besides longevity and staying true to their roots, are the ever-growing winemaking community they've built around Le Vin de Mes Amis and their continued dedication to making wine that's accessible to everyone. Jean-Baptiste takes pride in the fact that they limit the international export of their wine, preferring instead to introduce it to people from the village. "They can appreciate it clearly without the intellectual discourse often associated with natural wine, because what's important is to drink wine with your heart and your gut, not just with your head," remarks J-B with a smile.

Later that evening, we grab a few seats at one of the long communal tables, dressed in white tablecloths and overflowing with wine from every producer at the fair. Charlotte quickly warns us not to get too attached to any particular bottle because there is an unwritten rule at the annual Le Vin de Mes Amis dinner: every bottle on your table should be shared with a neighbor. This means that, every once in a while, you will see a rosy-cheeked guest from another table approach yours, offering a bottle in exchange for one from your lot. Then a few minutes later, you will rise from your chair and do the same, like some kind of natural-wine white-elephant gift exchange, until no bottle and no stranger remains.

4. Charlotte and Jean-Baptiste's son Isaac.

4

LATE SUMMER STUFFED GARDEN VEGETABLES

SERVES 2–4

This is David's take on a dish of tomates farcies (stuffed tomatoes) Zev enjoyed during a late-summer visit to Charlotte and Jean-Baptiste's house. A Southern French classic from none other than the queen and king of the South, this recipe can be made with whatever vegetable you may encounter while taking a stroll through your garden or local market. Have fun with it—mix and match plump tomatoes, seasonal peppers, and rugosa, butternut, and patty pan squashes!

INGREDIENTS

- 1 **cup** ricotta
- ¼ **cup** grated pecorino
- 2 large eggs
- 4 **tbs** chopped parsley
- Salt and black pepper
- 1 **lb** lean ground pork
- 1 **tbs** ground sage
- ¼ **cup** plus 1 tbs Parmigiano Reggiano
- ¼ **cup** plus 1 tbs breadcrumbs
- 1 rugosa or centercut squash
- 2 medium patty pan squashes (softball size) or medium yellow zucchini
- 2 summer squashes
- 3 various small sized sweet peppers
- 3 large tomatoes
- 1 **tbs** extra-virgin olive oil, plus additional to finish
- Additional Parmigiano Reggiano and pecorino to finish

INSTRUCTIONS

1. Preheat the oven to 350°F.

2. In a small bowl, mix together the ricotta, pecorino, 1 of the eggs, 2 tbs of the parsley, and a pinch of salt and pepper. Place in the refrigerator while you prepare the pork mixture.

3. In another large bowl, combine the ground pork, sage, the remaining egg, ¼ cup Parmigiano Reggiano, ¼ cup breadcrumbs, the remaining 2 tbs parsley, and a pinch of salt and pepper. Place in the refrigerator while you prepare the vegetables.

4. Split the long squashes lengthwise and cut the cap off the round squashes. Use a spoon to remove the seeds. Do the same with the tomatoes.

5. Stuff the tomatoes with the ricotta mixture and generously fill the squash and peppers with the ground pork mixture. Use a spoon to shape the stuffing neatly.

6. Place all the pork-stuffed vegetables in a baking dish or on a baking sheet. Drizzle with olive oil and the 1 tbs Parmigiano Reggiano and 1 tbs breadcrumbs. Place the tomatoes on a separate baking sheet.

7. Place both sets of vegetables in the oven. Bake the ricotta-filled tomatoes about 15 minutes, until they reach an internal temperature of 145°F. Bake the pork-filled squashes and peppers about 30 minutes, until they reach an internal temperature of 160°F.

8. Arrange all the vegetables nicely on your favorite platter. Garnish with more grated cheese and a drizzle of olive oil. Serve hot, cold, or at room temperature.

ITALY

REGIONS

Friuli
Trentino—Alto Adige
Emilia-Romagna
The Veneto
Tuscany
Lazio
Sicily

A Brief History of Natural Wine in Italy

The splintered origins of the natural-wine movement in Italy mirror the country's dizzying geopolitical evolution. Spanning over 4,000 years, the history of winemaking in Italy is rich, originating with the Etruscans who developed viticulture before being conquered by the Romans, who further spread the practice throughout their vast empire. Following the fall of the Romans, the Italian peninsula was divided into various kingdoms, duchies, and territories, which contributed to the diverse cultural and regional identities the country is known for today.

After centuries of political instability and division, the unification of Italy was finally completed in 1861. The abolishment of the monarchy in 1946 led to the establishment of the Italian Republic and the adoption of a new constitution. It would eventually grant special semiautonomous status to five regions to preserve their unique cultural and linguistic identities: Trentino–Alto Adige, Friuli Venezia Giulia, Valle d'Aosta, Sicily, and Sardinia. Despite all this, Italy's borders as we know them were not finalized until 1954 with the annexation of Trieste.

This cultural fragmentation is reflected in the emergence of the Italian natural-wine movement, which, unlike in France, did not gain momentum largely around a single group like that of Marcel Lapierre, Jules Chauvet, and Jacques Néauport. Rather, the first wave of Italian natural winemakers formed in clusters, each influenced by their unique regional practices and philosophies.

The Second World War had a profound impact on the Italian countryside, with the destruction of farmland and an acceleration of rural exodus, as many searched for better opportunities in cities. In the years that followed, the Italian government implemented a series of initiatives to revitalize the countryside. These included the redistribution of land from large estates to small farmers, the codification of *agriturismo* (a form of agricultural tourism), and the creation of the Denominazione di Origine Controllata (DOC) in 1963 and the Denominazione di Origine Controllata e Garantita (DOCG) in 1980. Inspired by the French AOC system, both these systems aimed to protect regional wine identities and make Italian wines more competitive domestically and internationally.

Both *denominazione* systems worked to a certain extent; however, by the 1980s and 1990s, the demand for wines made with international grape varietals like cabernet sauvignon, merlot, and chardonnay had skyrocketed. Frustrated with the rigidity of the two systems and eager to produce wines with broader commercial appeal, many Italian winemakers ditched the DOC and DOCG to experiment with international varietals. This gave rise to Super Tuscans, a new category of wines that blended traditional Sangiovese with international varietals. While the rapid and widespread success of these wines led to the introduction, in 1992, of the more flexible Indicazione Geografica Protetta (IGT) category, it also encouraged winemakers to uproot and replace indigenous Italian varietals, some of which had been cultivated for centuries. This shift contributed to a homogenization of wine styles and a loss of regional diversity across the country.

By the 1990s and early 2000s, a countermovement began to take hold, with pioneering winemakers in different pockets of the country rejecting industrial winemaking methods in favor of a more natural approach and ripping out international grapes planted by their parents. Early proponents of the Italian natural-wine movement included winemakers Joško Gravner, Stanislao "Stanko" Radikon, and Dario Prinčič (p.176) in Friuli Venezia Giulia; Elisabetta Foradori (p.184) in Trentino–Alto Adige; Angiolino Maule at La Biancara in the Veneto; Elena Pantaleoni and Stefano Bellotti in Piedmont; Giovanna Tiezzi and Stefano Borsa of Pacina in Tuscany; and Frank Cornelissen (p.222) and Arianna Occhipinti in Sicily.

As the movement gained momentum around the world in the early 2000s, the country's independent clusters of natural winemakers banded together in 2001, starting with wine distributor Luca Gargano's Triple "A" movement (*Agricoltori, Artigiani e Artisti*), or Agriculturalists, Artisans, Artists. In 2004, natural-wine trailblazers Stanko Radikon, Angiolino Maule, Fabrizio Niccolaini, and Giampiero Bea teamed up to create Consortium ViniVeri, a group of winemakers from different Italian regions and Slovenia. ViniVeri also hosts Italy's longest-running natural-wine fair. By 2006, Angiolino Maule had parted ways with ViniVeri to establish VinNatur, an association that hosts events across Europe, representing natural winemakers from around the world.

Today, Italy boasts twenty distinct winemaking regions, each rich with its own unique winemaking techniques and culinary traditions. With more than 350 authorized grape varietals and plenty of affordable land, Italy offers endless opportunities for exploration and natural-wine discoveries.

1. Flour dusting left behind after a pasta-making session.

IT

Friuli Venezia Giulia

The easiest way to understand Friuli Venezia Giulia, Friuli for short, is to think of it as a handsewn quilt. Tucked between the Adriatic Sea to the south, Slovenia to the east, and Austria to the north, Italy's northeastern most province has seen its borders stretched, ripped, and mended time and again. Over the course of its history, Friuli has been occupied by the Slavs, Ottomans, Venetians, Austrians, French, and Romans, effectively transforming the region into a diverse patchwork of landscapes and cultures. Today, four languages besides Italian remain in use in various pockets of the region: Friulian, Slovene, German, and Venetian.

Geographically speaking, Friuli's vineyards are divided into several subregions, including the imposing Grave del Friuli to the west, as well as the smaller, hilly regions of Collio and Colli Orientali del Friuli to the east. Characterized by alluvial soil made up of gravel and vast, tractor-accessible plains, Grave del Friuli is prime real-estate for commercial wineries. On the eastern side, the landscape is dominated by rolling hills and towering mountain ranges such as the Carnic Alps. Here high-altitude vineyards benefit from cooler temperatures, which, in turn, help to preserve acidity and freshness in the grapes. In Collio and Colli Orientali del Friuli, the soil, known as *ponca*, is the Adriatic's former seabed. A blend of sandstone and marl, it imparts the wines with pronounced minerality.

Like the rest of Italy, Friuli's winemaking in the twentieth century was greatly influenced by global trends, leading to the introduction of international varietals like merlot, cabernet sauvignon, sauvignon blanc, and chardonnay, which were often blended with native varietals like friulano, ribolla gialla, and malvasia.

Despite the destruction brought by countless wars, occupations, and even natural disasters, Friuli has never abandoned its centuries-old winemaking traditions. In fact, one might argue that the region's need to constantly rebuild and adapt has been a driver behind the modern winemaking revolutions it birthed.

In the 1960s, winemaker Mario Schiopetto introduced temperature-controlled fermentations in stainless steel tanks, which protected wines from oxidation and bacterial infections. Schiopetto's innovation resulted in crystal-clear, angular white wines that became the region's calling card, along with the fuller-bodied white wines aged in French barrels. Friuli's biggest winemaking revolution, however—one that would reverberate across the world and propel wine into the zeitgeist—wouldn't take root until the 1990s.

While orange wine, also known as skin-contact or amber wine, has a rich history that traces back thousands of years to the Republic of Georgia, its modern resurgence can largely be attributed to a small group of Friulian winemakers that included Joško Gravner, Stanislao Radikon, and Dario Prinčič. Despite its ubiquitous popularity at the time of this writing, orange wine wasn't an overnight success story. (The time is spring 2024, New York City, and if you close your eyes and listen closely, you can hear the sound of a thousand orange-wine glasses being poured in unison. And if you listen even closer, you can hear an even smaller murmur—the unmistakable sound of a server's soul dying as they explain what orange wine is for the hundredth time.) Initially, the orange wines coming out of Friuli faced mixed reactions because of their unconventional style, deep amber color, and departure from the mainstream clear-hued, crisp white wines pioneered by Mario Schiopetto. But gradually, they gained recognition among a niche audience of natural-wine aficionados, eventually becoming the standard for skin-contact winemaking around the world.

In the next few pages, we'll visit one of the godfathers of the orange-wine revolution, winemaker Dario Prinčič, whose vintages have become benchmarks of high-quality, age-worthy orange wines. The rabbit pasta served by Dario and his wife, Franca, alongside these wine, is a testament to the region's *cucina povera* (literally, kitchen or cuisine of the poor) and polyglot history. (*Biechi*, also known as *blecs* in the local Friulian, means "little tongues," like the shape of the pasta.)

1. Winemaker Dario Prinčič's grandson Jan enjoys a cherry.

Azienda Agricola Dario Prinčič

DARIO PRINČIČ

1

Back in 2018, armed with a rental car, a notebook, and a few cameras, Steph and Xavier traveled to Oslavia, a small northeastern Italian village bordering Slovenia, to meet with a few winemakers. After four days of hard work spent cooking and drinking with them, they put together a loose proposal for a cookbook about natural wine. It would eventually become the book you're holding in your hands today.

Four years after that first trip, we find ourselves once again driving along SP17, the strada that stretches out through Oslavia and eventually loops back through via Vellone dell'Acqua, into the town of Gorizia. Considered by many as the cradle of the modern orange-wine revolution, the area is home to some of the world's most well-known skin-contact wine producers, such as Joško Gravner, Stanislao "Stanko" Radikon, and the man we've come to see today, Dario Prinčič.

Rolling into the driveway, memories from that first trip come flooding back: the sprawling views that straddle Italy and Slovenia, the large stone etched with the winemaker's last name, and the menacing sound of Dario's massive, fluffy white dog barking at us. Amidst the ruckus, the winemaker greets us, his demeanor stern. Bearing the marks of years working in Friuli's sun-drenched vineyards, his face carries a serious note that adds gravitas to our symbolic return to Oslavia. A few steps behind Dario stands his friend Marko, a nervy punk rocker who will be our translator for the day.

Walking inside the house, we are immediately intrigued by a large modernist abstract landscape hanging on a wall near the entrance to the cellar. Territory of Orange Wine is painted across the blood-orange-colored soil, and etched on the bright green hills are the words *rebula* on one side, *ribolla gialla* on the other, referring to the Slovenian and Italian names for the region's star native grape. "Beautiful," whispers Xavier as we follow Dario and Marko through the threshold of the cellar, revealing large Slovenian oak *foudres* and casks.

Once inside, it doesn't take long for Dario's serious facade to come down, and for his

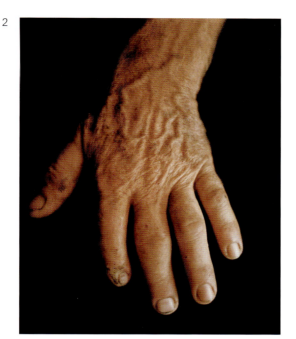

1. Winemaker Dario Prinčič
2. A lifetime in the vines has left its mark on Dario's hands
3. Dario enjoys lunch after a long tasting.

boyish side to emerge, much to the dismay of Marko, who inevitably blushes every time he is forced to translate one of Dario's silly quips. Every time we joke among ourselves in English, the winemaker's eyes light up, leading us to believe he understands a lot more English than he prefers to let on. This ambiguity manages to make the legendary winemaker even more compelling.

Dario grew up in Oslavia, among the same vines he tends today, on the estate established by his family in 1933. When he took over from his father in 1988, he chose to abandon the use of chemicals and transitioned to organic farming, incorporating some biodynamic methods. Five years later, Dario decided to start making wine himself instead of selling his grapes to local wineries. Around the same time, less than three kilometers north on SP17, winemakers Joško Gravner and Stanislao Radikon were beginning to experiment with macerated white wines (more on that on p.174).

Pouring us a few ounces of *ribolla gialla*, Dario recalls how vapid his wines tasted once he tried his neighbors' white macerations. "My wines felt like Coca-Cola," he says. That revelation had a domino effect. By the beginning of the new millennium, Dario's entire production consisted of skin-macerated wines.

Orange wine has experienced such a meteoric rise over the past decade that, for many, it's what first comes to mind when they hear the words natural wine. This makes it hard to grasp the challenges Dario and his Oslavian peers faced in the early days, when trying to persuade people to buy their skin-contact wines. However, the history of natural wine is, if nothing else, a story of underdogs rising to the top.

The winemaker gestures for us to take a sip of his *ribolla gialla* cuvée, which spends twenty days on the skins before being pressed. "Now this," he says, swishing the wine around his mouth, "it feeds you." Indeed, with its vibrant minerality, raspy tannins, deep texture, and complex aromas, Dario's *ribolla gialla*, like the rest of his skin-contact white wines, is as hearty as a Friulian feast.

Generally speaking, Dario's wines are a lot like Dario himself—initially austere, they eventually reveal themselves to be vibrant and full of life. Both his white and red wines usually boast high alcohol levels that the winemaker delicately balances with a desirable amount of volatile acidity, making them perfect candidates for ageing. Some of his red wines, like the cabernet sauvignon, are even aged up to ten years in barrels, during which time they take on oolong-like characteristics.

For lunch, we are joined by Dario's wife, Franca, and their two sons, Andrea and Marco. Both robust and burly, the brothers work diligently alongside their father in the vines and cellar. As Franca drops a plate of prosciutto on the table, Andrea pours himself a generous glass of ruby-colored macerated pinot grigio before brusquely setting the bottle back down. The loud thud hits us like a gust of fresh air.

Natural wine is paysan wine, that is to say, wine made by farmers. That was the central idea that guided us to Friuli all those years ago when this book was nothing but a seedling in our minds. Exhausted by the growing hype and pompous discourse surrounding natural wine and whether its popularity would persist, we wanted to show that natural wine, first and foremost, existed outside the context of cities, expensive wine bars, and Instagram feeds. We thought, what better place to showcase this dichotomy than the epicenter of the orange-wine revolution, since it's a style intricately linked with natural wine's growing popularity.

Now, finding ourselves back where this book journey began, we hoped for some grand revelation that would tie everything together and prove once and for all that natural wine is more than just a fad. But in that moment, sharing a meal with a family of winemakers—whom Steph describes as carbon copies of her uncles and cousins, a raucous bunch of lumberjacks and hunters—we experience something closer to taking a long exhale.

As we continue to drink bottles of wine without the preciousness we would apply back home in New York, questions about natural wine's longevity feel utterly pointless. Sure, the porch-pounder orange wines that have overflowed the market in recent years might eventually fall out of fashion, but if Dario's skin macerations are any example, we can rest assured that the movement has great ageing potential.

4

WINERY   IT

4. Franca showers her pasta with a healthy dose of grated Parmigiano Reggiano.

5. *Salute!*

5

RABBIT BIECHI

SERVES 4-6

Spend enough time in Italy, and you'll hear about a new pasta shape almost every day. Specific to the Friuli region, biechi, also known as blecs, is an irregularly shaped triangle pasta crafted from a mixture of buckwheat and regular wheat flours. When cooking this dish for their guests, Dario and Franca like to divide and conquer. She hand-makes her biechi using flours from a nearby mill, located just across the border in Slovenia, while Dario sets the rabbit to cook for hours while he's giving a tour of the cellar. The fresh pasta then cooks in the rabbit fat with a shower of finely grated cheese and black pepper, resulting in a dish that feels a lot like rustic cacio e pepe with a side of fall-off-the-bone rabbit.

INGREDIENTS

Special equipment: Pasta roller

Biechi
2 large eggs
1 large egg yolk
1 tbs extra-virgin olive oil
1 cup all-purpose flour, plus additional for dusting
½ cup buckwheat flour
Semolina flour, for dusting

Rabbit
1 whole rabbit (1½-2 lbs), cut into 6 pieces
Salt and black pepper
¼ cup extra-virgin olive oil
1 medium yellow onion, thinly sliced
½ cup dry white wine
2 cups chicken broth

To Assemble
½ cup (1 stick) unsalted butter
3 cups freshly grated Parmigiano Reggiano, plus additional for serving
Black pepper

INSTRUCTIONS

1. **For the biechi:** In a small bowl, whisk to combine the whole eggs, egg yolk, and olive oil.

2. Pour both flours onto a clean surface. With your hands, carefully shape the flour into a well and place the egg mixture in the center. Using a fork, slowly incorporate the flour into the egg mixture, beating gently until a shaggy dough begins to form. Knead the dough by hand until the consistency becomes more or less regular. Wrap the dough in plastic wrap and rest it for at least 1 hour and up to 4 hours.

3. To roll out and shape the pasta dough, it is always best to work in batches to avoid the pasta sheets drying. Set up the pasta roller on the widest possible setting. Cut the dough into 4 pieces, carefully wrapping and setting aside 3 pieces so they don't dry out. Flatten 1 piece of dough with your hands or with a rolling pin to about ⅓ inch thick, then carefully feed it through the roller. Roll it on the same setting once more. Continue rolling the dough through the machine, reducing the settings by one notch each time, until the dough is thin enough that you can begin to see your work surface through it.

4. Cut the pasta sheet into irregular 3-inch triangles. Place the biechi pieces on a baking sheet, lightly dust with semolina flour, and let rest for at least 30 minutes. Repeat the process with the remaining dough.

5. **For the rabbit:** Pat the rabbit pieces dry with a paper towel. Season with salt and pepper. Heat 2 tbs of the olive oil in a large Dutch oven set over medium-high heat. Working in batches, if needed, add the rabbit pieces and sear until golden, 3 to 5 minutes on each side. Transfer the seared rabbit to a plate. Don't wipe out the Dutch oven.

6. Add the onion to the Dutch oven and reduce the heat to medium, then cook, stirring occasionally, until just golden, about 10 minutes. Pour in the white wine and stir to remove

any bits that have stuck to the bottom of the pot. Continue to cook until the liquid is reduced by half, about 2 minutes.

7. Return the rabbit to the Dutch oven. Add the broth and bring to a simmer over medium-high heat. Turn the heat down to low, cover the pot, and cook until the meat is tender, about 90 minutes to 2 hours. Transfer the rabbit to a plate and cover with foil to keep warm. Don't drain the cooking liquid.

8. **To assemble:** Add the biechi along with the butter and Parmigiano Reggiano to the Dutch oven. Cook, stirring occasionally, until the pasta is al dente and the cheese and liquid have emulsified, 3 to 4 minutes. Divide the pasta onto plates and top with a piece of rabbit. Finish with additional Parmigiano Reggiano and pepper.

Trentino–Alto Adige

1. (Left) Zev, Elisabetta, and Steph beneath the towering Dolomites, discussing the winemaker's pergola vineyards.

One of Italy's five autonomous regions, Trentino–Alto Adige is, as its name suggests, composed of two distinct areas that are autonomous from each other: Alto Adige to the north and Trentino to the south. The easiest way to find your bearings is to follow the Adige River, which unites both subregions. The Adige rises in the Alps, near the border between Italy, Austria, and Switzerland, and flows through the Trentino–Alto Adige region before crossing over to the Veneto, where it eventually spills into the Adriatic Sea.

Also known as South Tyrol (or Südtirol in Austrian German), Alto Adige is dominated by the jagged peaks of the Dolomite Mountains and the Alps, which provide the region with a cooler continental climate and soils that vary among limestone, granite, and volcanic. Culturally, parts of the region feel more like Austria than Italy. Similarly to Friuli Venezia Giulia, Trentino–Alto Adige's borders are more smudged than precisely drawn, with many of its residents considering them arbitrary.

Follow the river farther south until Alto Adige's jagged peaks give way to Trentino's gentler mountains and hills, with the exception of the Dolomite's offshoot, Brenta Dolomiti, located just outside Mezzolombardo, where winemaker Elisabetta Foradori resides. Here, the warmer Mediterranean climate takes over and the soil turns sandy.

Vineyard elevation varies widely, but most of the region's vineyards are steep, which made it difficult for commercial wineries that favor tractor farming and harvesting over the back-breaking work of hand harvesting to establish roots. Instead, the region favored cooperatives, which provided small-scale grape growers with a stable source of income by purchasing their grapes. However, these cooperatives fell victim to international trends of the twentieth century, and winemakers began uprooting many of their native varietals in favor of planting high-demand, high-yielding grapes like chardonnay, pinot noir, and merlot.

In recent decades, efforts from a few small-scale, natural wineries have led to a resurgence of the region's almost-forgotten indigenous grapes: teroldego, lagrein, schiava, marzemino, nosiola, and groppello.

In the following pages, you will meet the queen of teroldego, Elisabetta Foradori, a true visionary whose outside-the-box thinking and steadfast determination proved that her region's native grapes were capable of greatness. The vibrant zucchini soup she effortlessly whipped up for us on a scorching afternoon reflects her ethos that less is often more.

IT   WINERY

Azienda Agricola Foradori

ELISABETTA FORADORI

1

"Beautiful," says Xavier, stating the obvious as we find ourselves enveloped by the dramatic, rocky cliffs of northern Italy's Dolomites. By now, the frequency with which Xavier will turn around and say "beautiful" has become somewhat of a running joke during our travels. He's never really wrong, but this time, "beautiful" doesn't quite capture it.

The Dolomites began forming 250 million years ago during the Triassic period, when vast shallow seas covered the region and dinosaurs roamed parts of Italy. Over time, the accumulation of marine sediments, which solidified into limestone, and the collision of the African and European tectonic plates, sculpted the spires, towers, cliffs, and pinnacles we know today.

The landscape here isn't just beautiful—it's humbling. Its grandeur shifts your perspective, prompting you to contemplate what came before

2

184

3

1. A few different cuvées enjoyed over lunch express the broad variety of styles made at Foradori.

2. Elisabetta picks green zucchini from her garden, set in between rows of vines.

3. Drawings featuring the names of Elisabetta's children, Myrtha and Theo.

and what lies ahead. For a fleeting moment, you set aside your worries and realize you're not the center of the universe. But it's not just landscapes that can evoke such feelings. Individuals who've profoundly shaped culture or witnessed significant waves of change can also instill a sense of humility. And if you're fortunate enough, as we are on this sun-drenched June morning, you might experience both simultaneously.

As we make our way toward the entrance of the Foradori estate, an impressive stone structure draped in vines set against the backdrop of the Dolomites, we see Elisabetta Foradori through the window, waving us inside. Her gray hair pulled back, wearing an apron and emerald-green earrings, the winemaker is even more beautiful in person than she is in photos. But beyond her appearance, it is her presence that is even more striking. A pioneer of biodynamics and a champion of indigenous varietals and traditional winemaking techniques, Elisabetta's contribution to the natural-wine movement in Italy and abroad cannot be overstated. Along with her other contemporaries like Stefano Bellotti of Cascina degli Ulivi and Elena Pantaleoni of La Stoppa, the winemaker has paved the way for many young winemakers starting out today. Smart, funny, and cynical, she is the kind of person you could sit with and listen to all day. Just like the Dolomites, her presence humbles.

Born into a winemaking family in Italy's Trentino region, Elisabetta found herself thrust into winemaking after her father's unexpected passing. Determined to revitalize the winery and honor her region's viticultural heritage, Elisabetta took some big swings.

Starting in the late 1990s, the young winemaker began converting her vineyards to biodynamic farming, completing the project in 2002. At that time, the prevailing trend in Italy was to replace relatively unknown indigenous varietals with highly esteemed French grapes like merlot and cabernet sauvignon. In a bold and controversial move, Elisabetta opted to remove all foreign vines and replant native grapes like teroldego, aiming to highlight their potential for crafting wines of exceptional character and complexity. While this decision may seem obvious today, it was unprecedented at the time. "I was passionate, and I had a vision," she reflects.

Elisabetta leads us to another building, down a set of stairs, and into a high-ceilinged room filled with her legendary clay amphoras. Crafted in Spain by a potter named Juan Padilla, Foradori's teardrop-shaped amphoras facilitate a gentle exchange of oxygen during the ageing process, enhancing the expression of terroir. Unlike their Georgian counterparts, Elisabetta's amphoras are stored aboveground.

Returning upstairs, Elisabetta pours us a few glasses of wine to taste. The first wine, a macerated pinot grigio, is barely orange, translucent. "After about seven months on the skins in amphoras, the color will begin to fade," she explains. Elisabetta's white wines undergo maceration but express themselves very differently from those made in Friuli. The nosiola variety offers delicate extraction during maceration, resulting in a wine with just a hint of grip on the palate. Meanwhile, the pinot grigio displays a clearer extraction of color and tannin, yielding an incredibly complex and deep wine. The reds possess a certain robustness, yet ageing in amphoras seems to soften the tannins to a barely noticeable level. Finesse is the defining characteristic of all Foradori wines. They're not timid or small, but they'll never beat you over the head either. The bottles are adorned with classic-looking labels, the wines aren't cloudy at all, and the nose and palate exhibit no flaws. For someone unfamiliar with her work, they might even appear conventional.

Elisabetta acknowledges feeling dismissed by some younger winemakers who consider her too old-school and criticize her minimal use of sulfur, arguing she isn't doing enough for the natural-wine movement. However, she's not interested in engaging in debates solely for the sake of ideology. "There are many good new projects out there. I don't like the term 'natural wine,'" she asserts. "I prefer to speak of artisanal wine rooted in identity, place, and people."

Elisabetta hands us a book. With beautiful illustrations embossed on a light woven-fabric cover, *The Pentagon: Memoirs on the Agricultural Philosophy Understanding of Vine and Wine* is a collection of philosophical writings on biodynamics penned by her late husband, the German writer and naturalist, Rainer Zierock. "Keep it," she says, displaying the generosity of someone who has spent a lifetime developing knowledge meant to serve future generations.

In recent years, with her children joining the estate, Foradori has taken an accelerated shift toward biodiversity. The winemaker describes her approach as a mix of science and spirituality. "You have to observe, be present, and consider everything as part of a larger global process," she explains.

Her sons, Emilio and Theo, have taken over most of the winemaking side of the operation,

4

5

while daughter Myrtha, after gaining experience in the United States and Quebec, is creating biodiversity in the vineyard with a large vegetable garden rising between the pergolas.

Meanwhile, Elisabetta has ventured into cheesemaking, embracing rich traditions older than herself high up in the Dolomites, where her Tyrol Grey cows graze. Amidst the unpredictability of nature and fermentations, she finds herself humbled once more, this time by a totally different beast.

6

4. Elisabetta takes a break by the spring.

5. The best zucchini you've ever had.

6. The view from Elisabetta's kitchen.

ZUCCHINI SOUP WITH FRESH CHEESE

SERVES 4

Since this soup is so simple, its success largely hinges on the quality of the zucchini. When Elisabetta made it for us back in Mezzolombardo, she led us to one of the vegetable gardens tended by her daughter, Myrtha Zierock. This particular garden, planted behind the house between rows of towering vines in pergola, overflowed with zucchini plants. After picking a few bright ones, Elisabetta brought us back to the kitchen, where she introduced us to some of the alpine cheeses she crafts using raw milk from the estate's Tyrol Grey cows, an ancient alpine breed that grazes in nearby mountainous fields. To garnish this soup, the winemaker used a dollop of homemade labneh-like alpine cheese called Alpneh, but Greek yogurt or labneh work well too—just make sure to use peak-season zucchini for the soup.

INGREDIENTS

- 6 medium zucchini, roughly chopped
- 2 spring onions, white and green parts, roughly chopped
- 1 tbs salt
- 4 pinches black pepper
- Extra-virgin olive oil, to finish
- 4 tbs labneh (or Greek yogurt)
- 4 tsp torn mint
- Edible flowers to garnish (optional)

INSTRUCTIONS

1. In a medium pot, add the zucchini, spring onions, salt, and ½ cup of water and bring to a simmer over medium-high heat. Cook until the zucchini is tender, about 8 minutes, and let it cool down slightly.

2. Using an immersion blender, pulse the zucchini mixture until smooth. (Alternatively, you can carefully transfer to a blender and blend until smooth.) Bring the soup back to a simmer. Taste and adjust the seasoning with salt.

3. Divide the soup among 4 bowls and top each one with a pinch of pepper, a drizzle of olive oil, and 1 tbs labneh. Garnish with 1 tsp torn mint leaves and, if using, edible flowers. Serve immediately.

Emilia-Romagna

Many of Italy's most famous culinary exports hail from Emilia-Romagna, a northern Italian region stretching from the Po River Valley in the north to the Apennine Mountains in the south: Parmigiano Reggiano, Prosciutto di Parma, Bolognese sauce, and, of course, the now-reviled Lambrusco.

After reaching the height of its popularity in the 1970s, the sparkling red wine experienced a rapid fall from grace due to the mass production of cheap, syrupy versions that lacked the complexity and finesse of its predecessors. In many ways, Lambrusco has become Emilia-Romagna's scarlet letter, a stigma the region struggles to shake off. However, unlike the Veneto, where the tides of prosecco's dominance have been slow to turn, Emilia-Romagna has established itself as a stronghold for natural wine.

Much of this transformation can be credited to the efforts of Elena Pantaleoni of La Stoppa, arguably one of the most influential pioneers in Emilia-Romagna's natural-wine scene. The winemaker has played a crucial role in preserving and promoting the region's indigenous grape varieties, notably barbera, bonarda, and malvasia, while also advocating for biodynamic farming practices and traditional winemaking techniques. Pantaleoni's wines have become emblematic not only of the natural-wine movement but Emilia-Romagna's potential as a world-class wine region, inspiring other winemakers to create wines that reflect a true sense of place and authenticity.

Emilia-Romagna encompasses a diverse range of landscapes, from hills and plains to coastal areas. The foothills of the Apennines, with their limestone-based soil, lend mineral nuances to the wines. Here, cooler temperatures and significant diurnal temperature variation enhance the acidity and complexity of the grapes. Conversely, the fertile blend of clay, sand, and silt found in the plains of the Po River Valley, coupled with warmer temperatures, yields riper, more fruit-forward wines.

While inexpensive Lambrusco continues to cast a shadow over the region, Emilia-Romagna's winemaking landscape is teeming with a new generation of natural winemakers dedicated to expressing their region's terroir. Once under the assault of French varietals, vineyards are being replanted with local grapes like albana, trebbiano, pignoletto, malvasia, barbera, and bonarda. These winemakers are also exploring old methods anew, producing vibrant *pét-nats* and deeply hued skin-macerated white wines that rival those of their Friulian neighbors to the east. Winemakers like Federico Orsi, located just outside Bologna, are even reviving long-lost traditions such as *vino perpetuo*. Since 2009, Orsi has been crafting both white and red cuvées by fermenting a blend of freshly harvested grapes in a tank partially filled with wines from previous vintages, resulting in a multivintage perpetual wine that doubles as a love letter to the terroir of Emilia-Romagna.

In this section, you'll become acquainted with Sebastian Van de Sype, a Belgian racecar engineer who left everything behind to pursue a brighter future for Lambrusco. While the accompanying recipe for osso buco isn't native to Emilia-Romagna, its origins as a way to transform less desirable meat cuts into a delicious dish resonate with the winemaker's mission to rehabilitate Lambrusco.

Sebastian Van de Sype Winery

SEBASTIAN & MARIEKE VAN DE SYPE

"I have a lot of former colleagues who come by the vineyard, and I always tell them, 'Look, this is my office now!'" exclaims a beaming Sebastian Van de Sype, the Belgian-born Ferrari aerospace engineer-turned-winemaker, as we reach the top of his steep vineyard nestled in Castelvetro di Modena in northern Italy. Despite being surrounded by verdant hills and forests, Sebastian's newfound slice of paradise comes with a built-in challenge: 90 percent of the grapes growing on Sebastian's five hectares of vines are Lambrusco, a grape that has become synonymous with cheap, sweet, and aggressively sparkling red wines.

Lambrusco did not always have such a bad reputation. In fact, Emilia-Romagna's native grape has such a long history (it was referenced in the first scientific encyclopedia, *Naturalis Historia* published in 77 CE) that it would be hard to accurately track all of its iterations. It is believed that the Etruscans, who lived across Italy from 900 BCE to 27 BCE when the Romans invaded, cultivated the grape in order to produce still red wine. Sparkling Lambrusco, on the other hand, appeared around the 1700s. It was fermented using the traditional method until the twentieth century, when winemakers began experimenting with different fermentation techniques. In the 1950s, they finally landed on the Charmat method, in which the second fermentation takes place in a large temperature-controlled metal tank instead of in the bottle. This change allowed winemakers to scale up their production, in turn leading to a drop in quality and price of the wines. As a result, Lambrusco became the biggest-selling import wine in the United States throughout the 1970s and 1980s. Consumer trends eventually changed and sales of Lambrusco have since continued to freefall.

So why would an engineer quit his high-paying job at Ferrari to make Lambrusco? Well, Sebastian Van de Sype is nothing if not

1

an ambitious dreamer who loves a challenge. "Growing up, I had three dreams," he says. "I wanted to have my own company, work in Formula 1, and end my life in a vineyard."

Sebastian spent a lot of his childhood hanging around his father, who was a true wine aficionado. Although his dad never made it a career, he was known among his friends for being a spectacular taster. One of those friends was a wine merchant named Frank Cornelissen, who would eventually become one of the most famous natural winemakers of our generation (see p.222). A typical evening for Sebastian's father and Frank would go something like this: Frank would show up at the Van de Sype house late at night, bottles in hand, and the two men would spend hours drinking and talking about everything from wine and music to politics. "I did everything not to go to bed when they were talking, because it was very interesting to listen to," Sebastian recalls. So the young man sat and listened while the men blind-tasted bottle after bottle. "Whenever somebody brought a bottle, it needed to be covered because it needed to be drunk in an unbiased way. It was really about what was in the glass," he adds.

Sebastian grew up to study aerospace engineering with a specialty in aerodynamics, and completed his master's degree working at Ferrari, in Modena, Italy. After his stint with the luxury carmaker, Sebastian returned to Belgium to start a family with his wife, Marieke, and founded a company specializing in business intelligence

2

1. Winemakers Sebastian and Marijke Van de Sype stroll the rolling hills above Modena where their vineyards lie.

2. Sebastian contemplating his Lambrusco.

and process management. In 2014, Sebastian was offered a job in Ferrari's Formula 1 aerodynamics department—his dream job. He sold his company and moved his wife and two children to Modena. But soon enough, he felt pulled toward his dream of becoming a winemaker. "I started to ride my motorbike around during my lunch breaks, and I just fell in love with where we were. I started tasting stuff and reading about the history. I started to really see the opportunity to do it here," says Sebastian.

When Sebastian told his old friend and mentor Frank Cornelissen that he wanted to become a winemaker, the Etna giant shut him down immediately. "He said don't do it," recounts Sebastian. "But I remember the hug he gave me at the end of that day. He looked me in the eyes and said, 'Maybe you're going to do it,' and I said, 'Yeah, maybe I'm going to do it.'" In 2020, Sebastian purchased four and a half hectares of vines planted mostly with Lambrusco gasparosso, except for a small parcel of trebbiano.

3. Speed bump ahead.

4. Marijke preparing glasses for tasting.

5. Winemaker Marijke Van de Sype.

3

4

Back in Sebastian's vineyard, where we are coincidentally joined by two of our friends who are in town working on the movie *Ferrari*, Sebastian shows us a leaf pierced with a giant hole, the result of a recent hailstorm that has wreaked havoc on his vines. We catch a glimpse of his engineer's brain at work as he assesses the severity of the damage and what it might mean for his third vintage and his long-held dream. But then he turns around, and with a steadfast focus on the future, explains his plans to build a brand-new winery on the property in the coming years (he currently vinifies in a shared facility).

In his first and second vintages, Sebastian produced two cuvées of Lambrusco using the traditional method. "I want to go back to the old-style Lambrusco but do it in a clean way, with fine bubbles, balanced acidity, nice tension, and no defects," he says. Both the Rifermentato (on the lees) and Ancestrale (disgorged) are dry, complex, and, most importantly, eons away from the cloying wines that tarnished the Lambrusco name in the first place.

When we reach Sebastian a few months after our visit, he is on the other side of a very difficult harvest, where most of his production did not survive the hailstorm. Despite the hardships, the winemaker remains resolute in his ambition to bring Lambrusco back to its glory days. He is even hoping to turn the next generation on to the wines with a new Lambrusco rosato he has been working on. "My dream is that I won't have to discuss the term Lambrusco anymore, and that people start considering what's in their glass instead of judging it based on a name that got fucked by the industry."

5

OSSO BUCCO

SERVES 3–5

Osso Bucco is one of those quintessential Italian dishes that looks super impressive but actually requires very little effort once you've seared the meat. As it braises slowly, the marrow at the center of each veal shank melts into the sauce, imparting it with added richness and depth of flavor. For Sebastian and Marijke, it's the perfect choice to welcome visitors to their adoptive country while juggling a busy schedule. Serve it with a side of creamy polenta or a slice of country bread to soak up the sauce.

INGREDIENTS

1 veal shank (about 3 lbs), sliced into 5 pieces for osso bucco (ask your butcher)
Salt and black pepper
2 **tbs** all-purpose flour
2 **tbs** unsalted butter
3 medium carrots, finely diced
1 medium white onion, finely diced
1 celery stalk, finely diced
2 **cups** Lambrusco
3 **cups** tomato passata (or tomato puree)
1 **tsp** sugar
Lemon zest, for serving

INSTRUCTIONS

1. Preheat the oven to 300°F.

2. Pat the veal shank pieces dry and season both sides with salt and pepper. Shower the veal shank pieces with flour, and use your fingers to lightly rub it into the meat. (The flour will help put a nice crust on the veal and, once it's mixed in with the gelatin of the bone marrow, will help bind the sauce.)

3. Heat a large pan over medium-high heat. Add the butter and cook until it becomes frothy and starts browning, about 4 minutes. Add the veal shank pieces. (You should hear only a light sizzle when the meat hits the pan, so if it sizzles too much, remove from the heat and let the pan cool down slightly.) Cook for about 5 minutes until a golden-brown crust forms, swirling the pan every so often to avoid burning, then flip and cook on the other side, another 5 minutes. Transfer the osso bucco to a large Dutch oven. Don't wipe out the pan.

4. In the same pan over medium-low heat, add the carrots, onion, and celery. Gently sweat until the onion is translucent and the carrots have begun to soften, 4 to 5 minutes. Pour in the Lambrusco and stir, scraping up any bits that have stuck to the bottom of the pot. Cook for a few minutes, until the liquid has evaporated. Add the tomato passata, the sugar, a pinch of salt and pepper, and bring to a simmer, stirring occasionally to avoid burning.

5. Pour the tomato sauce over the veal pieces in the Dutch oven and transfer to the oven. Cook for 3 to 4 hours, until the meat is extremely tender. Remove from the oven and top with some grated lemon zest before serving.

The Veneto

When people think of the Veneto, romance usually comes to mind. This northern Italian province extends from the Alps down to the Adriatic Sea, where its capital, Venice, often considered one of the world's most romantic cities, floats gracefully on its waters. Near the region's western border lies the town of Verona, immortalized by William Shakespeare in several of his plays, including the tragic tale of Romeo and Juliet.

Long before becoming synonymous with honeymooners sipping prosecco while cruising Venice's canals in gondolas, the Veneto was a bustling trade hub. Venice's strategic position in the Adriatic Sea, at the nexus of major trade routes linking Europe and the East, including the Silk Road, established the region as a pivotal center for the exchange of goods like spices, silk, precious metals, and wine.

With a long-standing culture geared toward profit and a landscape defined by vast, tractor-friendly plains, it's hardly shocking that the Veneto has emerged as Italy's highest-producing wine region. But in the world of wine, too much of a good thing usually means it's bad. While the region produces a variety of wines using indigenous grapes like garganega, corvina, molinara, and rondinella, the prevalence of industrial wineries churning out enough prosecco to flood Venice under a sea of bubbles has resulted in a homogenization of its winemaking practices.

Prosecco isn't solely responsible for the gradual dilution of the Veneto's reputation. Another flagship Venetian creation, Amarone della Valpolicella, which soared to fame in the twentieth century, continues to polarize. Produced using the *appassimento* method, where grapes are dried before fermentation, Amarone is bold, potent, and boasts high alcohol levels that can overpower the palate. A single sip can feel akin to the Kool-Aid man bursting through a brick wall, obliterating any possible subtleties and nuances in its wake. For a while, the dominance of Amarone obscured the fact that corvina, molinara, and rondinella can yield fresher, more vibrant expressions in Valpolicella and Bardolino (although both styles run the risk of becoming flat and uninspired when produced on a large scale).

Made from Veneto-native garganega, Soave wines, especially those mass-produced for the market, have given the grape a reputation for being one-dimensional. Fortunately, in recent decades, natural winemakers like Filippo Filippi of Cantina Filippi and Angiolino Maule of La Biancara are using traditional and noninterventionist winemaking techniques to unleash garganega's full potential. Maule's garganega wines are moving examples of the grape's depth and complexity, revealing a purity of fruit and distinct minerality that mirrors the volcanic and limestone-rich soils of the Veneto.

In this section, you will meet Alessia and Stefano Bertaiola of Vini Sassara, newcomers dedicated to honoring their land's history through winemaking. During our visit, Alessia and her mother treated us to a feast that would impress even the most discerning Venetian culinary historian. From that meal, we chose a dish so delightful it still haunts our dreams.

Sassara Vini

ALESSIA & STEFANO BERTAIOLA

"Legend has it that this recipe appeared in the thirteen hundreds, when a soldier and a nymph fell in love, and while taking refuge from their enemies on the banks of the River Mincio, left behind a knotted yellow handkerchief as a symbol of their love," Alessia Bertaiola recounts, as she sets a plate of fresh Tortellini di Valeggio on the table. Filled with a blend of pork, beef, and veal, and simply dressed with butter and a shower of grana padano cheese, Alessia's perfectly knotted tortellini, like every other dish on the table, from the tortellini to the *salsa peará* (p.204), is served with a side of history.

Though Alessia and Stefano Bertaiola are only a few years into their winemaking journey with Sassara Vini, it's evident that their approach is deeply rooted in tradition. A visit to their fifteen-hectare estate, nestled in the hills of Valeggio sul Mincio, south of Lake Garda, feels like a crash course in the history of Verona. Much like today's menu, the couple's wines are a love letter to the region's heritage. "The biggest compliment for us is when people say that our wines taste of the land," Alessia says.

Stefano, a third-generation winemaker, was born and raised in Valeggio sul Mincio. After spending part of his adult life working in commercial wineries, he made the pivotal decision, in 2007, to assume ownership of the estate that had been in his family for over fifty years. Hailing from a small village just outside Valeggio and armed with a background in agricultural research and development, Alessia eventually joined Stefano on his journey toward crafting authentic wine. Having both previously worked in industrial settings, they decided to go the natural route. The duo swiftly converted the property to biodynamic farming, dedicating ten hectares to vines and the remaining five to olive groves and other trees.

In pursuit of a truer expression of their rich terroir (Sassara, in the local dialect, refers to a place rich in calcareous stones), they enlisted the help of Danilo Marcucci. An experienced winemaker, Danilo collaborates with various small-scale natural-wine producers throughout Italy, such as Furlani and Vini Rabasco, providing guidance on everything from biodynamic preparations to bottling.

1. Winemaker Alessia Bertaiola.
2. Lunch outside the winery at Vini Sassara.

2

The wines at Sassara Vini are vinified and packaged for pure enjoyment. Packed in clear bottles that allow the wine's color to come through in all its glory, the winery's nine cuvées showcase the natural-wine rainbow, from light white to light red. The white wines are fresh and high-toned, while the orange wines are delicately macerated and aromatic; the red wines are characterized by their lightness and see-through quality. It would be easy to dismiss these wines, with their vivid hues and playful labels, as trying to appeal to current market trends in natural wine. But this assumption misses the mark. Much like the food they cooked for us, the style of wines crafted by Alessia and Stefano are deeply rooted in history and tradition.

The province of Verona perhaps is better known for producing Amarone della Valpolicella, a relatively modern wine style that emerged in the twentieth century and gained international recognition. Made using the *appassimento* method, where grapes are dried before fermentation, Amarone yields deeply extracted, full-bodied red wines with pronounced flavors of dried fruits, spices, and a high alcohol content. In other words, Sassara Vini's wines represent the antithesis of Amarone.

Indeed, long before Amarone, there was Bardolino. Named after the town bordering Lake Garda, these red wines are known for their light

body, lively acidity, and gentle tannins—a stark contrast to the heaviness of Amarone. The history of Bardolino traces back to the Romans, who first planted vineyards in the region. Typically crafted from a blend of indigenous grape varieties such as corvina, rondinella, and molinara, Bardolino epitomizes the ancient winemaking traditions of the Veneto. And if there's one thing Alessia and Stefano love, it's tradition.

Today, they pride themselves on growing only grapes indigenous to the region, including red grapes like corvina, rossanella, rondinella, and white varietals like garganega, trebbiano, trebbianello, fernanda, malvasia, and moscato, to name a few. "Our vision for the future is to fully restore the ancient local vine varieties and craft wines in the tradition of our ancestors," says Alessia. "Flavorful wines that remind us where we came from."

As our lunch draws to a close, Stefano reaches for a bottle of Chiaretto Ciaro Rosso, a direct-press blend of traditional Bardolino grapes (corvina, rondinella, and molinara) and pours himself a glass before settling back into his chair. "When I drink our wines today, I don't think of natural wine. I just taste the wines of my youth—the ones my father used to make," he says, as a radiant grin spreads across his face.

3. Map of the vineyards in the region.

4. Tortellini di Valeggio.

5. Stefano walks outside the winery.

6. Stefano takes a rest in his kitchen before heading back out into the vineyard.

6

BOLLITO MISTO WITH PEARÀ SAUCE

SERVES 6–8

From the moment Alessia's pearà sauce touched our lips, we knew we'd found something special. From the Veronese dialect term for peppery, pearà typically accompanies bollito misto, which translates to mixed boil, referring to the method of cooking various cuts of meat in an aromatic broth. Made from breadcrumbs, grated cheese, broth from the cooking liquid, and lots of black pepper, this creamy sauce complements the richness of the meat perfectly. "The secret to making a great pearà sauce is time: the longer it cooks, the better it will be," advises Alessia. To this day, pearà, or bread sauce, as we've come to call it, remains one of the highlights of the many years we spent working on this book.

INGREDIENTS

Apple Mostarda
- 1 cup apple cider vinegar
- ¼ cup hard apple cider
- ½ cup sugar
- 1 piece fresh ginger (about 1 inch), grated
- 1 tsp salt
- ½ tsp black pepper
- ¼ large onion, finely diced
- 3 tbs yellow mustard seeds
- 1½ lbs tart apples, peeled and diced

Pearà Sauce
- ½ cup (1 stick) unsalted butter
- 1 cup finely grated stale bread
- 4 cups beef broth
- 1 tsp salt
- 1 tsp black pepper
- ¼ cup grated Grana Padano cheese

Bollito Misto
- 1 lb beef (cheek, brisket, or boneless shank)
- 1 chicken cut into 8 pieces
- 1 veal shank (about 2 lbs), sliced for osso bucco (ask your butcher)
- 1 medium onion, quartered
- 2 medium carrots, cut into 1-inch pieces
- 4 medium ribs celery, cut into 1-inch pieces
- 2 bay leaves
- 1 bunch thyme, tied with a string
- 2 tbs coriander seeds
- 1 tsp crushed white peppercorns
- 1 tbs salt, plus additional for seasoning
- ½ lb corned beef tongue
- 1 lb cotechino (or sweet Italian sausage)
- 1 cup beef broth (optional)
- Grated Grana Padano cheese, for serving
- Black pepper for seasoning

INSTRUCTIONS

1. **For the apple mostarda:** In a large pot set over high heat, combine the vinegar, cider, sugar, ginger, salt, and pepper and bring to a boil. Add the onion and mustard seeds, and lower the heat to medium. Cook until the onion is soft and translucent and the liquid is reduced by half, 10 to 15 minutes. Add the apples and cook until the mixture becomes soft and spreadable, another 15 to 20 minutes. If the mixture becomes dry as it cooks, add more cider to prevent burning. Remove from the heat and set aside. Serve warm or at room temperature.

2. **For the pearà sauce:** In a medium pot over low heat, melt the butter. Add the bread and stir to combine. Add the beef broth, salt, pepper and Grana Padano, and bring to a boil over medium heat. Reduce the heat to low and simmer for 2 hours, stirring often to avoid burning, until the sauce is reduced by half.

3. **For the bollito misto:** In a very large pot (a turkey roaster pot with lid would work), add the beef, chicken pieces, veal shank pieces, onion, carrots, celery, bay leaves, thyme, coriander seeds, white peppercorns, and the 1 tbs salt. Add enough cold water to cover everything by 1 inch. Bring to a boil over high heat, then reduce the heat down to low. Cover and simmer for 2 hours, occasionally skimming any undesirable foam, until the veal is fork-tender.

4. Add the corned beef tongue and cotechino. Add 2 cups of water (or 1 cup of water and 1 cup of beef broth, if using) and bring to a very slow simmer. Simmer on low until fork-tender, about 30 minutes. Taste the broth and adjust the seasoning with salt and pepper. Transfer the meat from the pot onto a cutting board and slice.

5. Divide the meats onto warm plates and serve with a dollop of apple mostarda and a generous serving of pearà sauce topped with grated Grana Padano. Serve the vegetables and broth in a bowl at the center of the table with a ladle.

y that makes you feel like anything is possible.
ng cypress trees reaching toward technicolor
has a way of making even the most realist of
behind and start over (à la *Under the Tuscan Sun*).
ve appeal of the land, the city of Florence, with
tiled skyline, makes an equally convincing appeal

ket-list destination for tourists trying to catch
id and his washboard-marble abs (among other
r one of the greatest eras of reinvention in his-
d a wave of artists and scientists whose defiance
de range of technological, scientific, and artistic
rld as we know it. It also brought about a period
rity for Tuscany during which wealthy families,
vards, bolstering the region's wine industry.

Tuscany owes much of its winemaking success to its natural disposition for viticulture. The Mediterranean climate, diverse soils—from the clay and limestone of Chianti to the sandy, gravelly terroir of Bolgheri—and rich winemaking heritage dating back to the Etruscans, around the eighth century BCE, have all played pivotal roles. The region is also home to several indigenous grape varietals: ciliegiolo, vernaccia, trebbiano, and, most notably, Sangiovese, whose acute ability to express terroir variations makes it the crown jewel of Italian grapes.

Sangiovese acts as the backbone of many well-known Tuscan wines, namely Chianti, Brunello di Montalcino, and Vino Nobile di Montepulciano. The more famous of the Sangiovese DOC, Chianti's reputation fell into disrepair in the 1960s as export markets ballooned and the industry shifted toward quantity over quality.

Around the same time, up in the hills of Maremma, a renaissance was brewing. Inhabited by a spirit of defiance and seeking to deviate from traditional Italian regulations, winemaker Marchese Mario della Rochetta, having replanted his vineyard with cabernet sauvignon and cabernet franc, began producing a Bordeaux-style red wine called Sassicaia. Della Rochetta's new wine quickly gained international acclaim. Shortly after, the term "Super Tuscan" was coined to describe red Tuscan wines made with French varietals. While the Super Tuscan craze elevated the reputation of Tuscan wine on the global stage, it ultimately encouraged producers to shift their focus toward international grape varieties at the expense of indigenous Tuscan grapes. The impulse to cash in on the trend also gave rise to a wave of cheap, over-extracted Super Tuscans that overshadowed the region's history of terroir-driven wines.

Since then, Tuscany has started to undergo another winemaking renaissance, driven by a rebellious group of natural winemakers. They are committed to showcasing the region's unique terroir with precision and finesse, through sustainable farming practices and minimal-intervention winemaking. Throughout the region, innovative winemakers are rediscovering the joys afforded by the region's native varietals like canaiolo, vernaccia, and ansonica.

In the Chianto Classico zone near Castelnuovo Berardenga, trailblazers like Giovanna Tiezzi and Stefano Borsa at Pācina eschew Chianti designations, preferring to operate outside the stifling bureaucracy of Italy's DOC system and to allow the grapes to speak for themselves.

In Maremma, the region that birthed Super Tuscan, Trentino star Elisabetta Foradori uses overlooked grapes like Alicante Bouschet and Alicante Nero to produce vibrant wines under the label Ampeleia.

In the following pages, you will meet the folks at La Ginestra, a collective whose countryside *agriturismo* presents a vision for the future of winemaking that prioritizes the preservation of biodiversity. Freshly prepared using ingredients grown on their land, the accompanying recipe is a testament to an old way of life made new again.

La Ginestra

DARIO NOCCI, MATTEO RINALDI & CO.

We're packed shoulder-to-shoulder in the back of a toy-size Fiat Panda, driven by Matteo Rinaldi of La Ginestra. Before us, acres upon acres of sprawling wheat fields punctuated by lush vineyards stretch beyond the horizon line, accentuating the expansive nature of the ninety-hectare, employee-owned winery and *agriturismo* located in the heart of Tuscany's Chianti Classico DOC.

The farm began in 1978, when a group of people rescued abandoned land under laws established by the Italian government after the Second World War. Postwar Italy's countryside saw significant decline as people moved to urban areas for better job opportunities, leaving many rural farms deserted. To rejuvenate these neglected lands, the Italian Civil Code allowed the government to allocate unclaimed, abandoned properties to new owners who would put them to productive use. "In the 1970s, a group of thirty-year-olds started looking for abandoned land in the area," says Matteo. "They found a five-hundred-hectare piece of land that had been completely abandoned and thought they could make something out of it. Thanks to that law, the owner was forced to rent it to them."

The collective initially operated La Ginestra as a goat farm and *agriturismo*. The concept of *agriturismo*, combining agriculture (*agricoltura*) and tourism (*turismo*), began in the 1960s. It helped farmers supplement their income by hosting tourists and providing accommodation and food typically produced on the farm. Recognizing its potential, the Italian government actively promoted *agriturismo* in the 1970s to support small-scale, family-run farms.

Having grown up in a small village ten minutes away from La Ginestra, Matteo is a great historian of the area. As we squeeze out of the Panda, he gestures, explaining the land's evolution. "When La Ginestra started, there were no vineyards, olive trees, bees, or cows. There were only grains and goats," he says.

While La Ginestra's goat cheese enterprise proved financially unsustainable, the *agriturismo* business thrived. The collective then began planting more crops, including grains, legumes, and fruit trees, and, in the 1990s, expanded into beekeeping and vines. Today, La Ginestra farms biodynamically and keeps a few cows and pigs, which are crucial to the farm's biodiverse ecosystem.

1

2

3

Matteo explains, "We approach the cows holistically—we don't take milk from them and only get some meat occasionally. We let the cows eat the grass, clean the fields, and enrich the soil with their manure."

We hop back in the Panda to meet winemaker Dario Nocci at the cellar. Comprising a series of small concrete structures, the cellar is stacked with barrels of wine at various stages of fermentation. Before joining La Ginestra, Dario honed his craft in Australia and Florence. Jumping from barrel to barrel like a kid at a jungle gym, Dario tells us about making his first wines without selective yeasts, sulfur, or filtration in 2012, a year after he joined La Ginestra. More than a decade later, the wines of La Ginestra are driven by the collective's creative spirit. While he produces classical-style Chianti, characterized by its tannic structure and leathery low tones, Dario also loves to experiment with macerations, amphora ageing, and pét-nats. Much like their label's signature snake, the resulting cuvées are full of twists and turns.

It is almost dinnertime by the time we return to the *agriturismo*, where La Ginestra's community spirit is on full display. A group of friends has arrived and is setting up a long table in the middle of the gravel driveway. There are kids playing, dogs running about, and smiles all

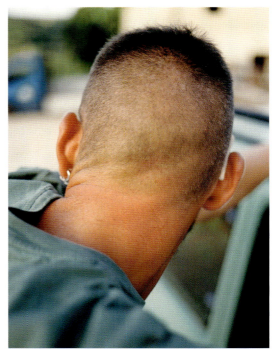

4

1. La Ginestra is more than just a winery: they grow wheat, olives, and raise animals in efforts to develop more biodiversity.

2. Beautiful cows at La Ginestra.

3. Farmer and winemaker Alessandro Bicchi in the cellar.

4. Alessandro looks back.

around. La Ginestra's chef, Cinzia, is bustling in the kitchen, preparing portions large enough to feed an army. Soon, she emerges with a massive pot of creamy tagliatelle with zucchini, which, as she mentions, grows in abundance this time of year.

Dishing out generous portions, Matteo lists the various products La Ginestra sells at the farmer's market alongside wine: honey, grains, flour, bread, pasta, baked goods, olive oil, salume, and even a marijuana-infused liqueur. "Since most farmers in this area already make their own wine and olive oil, most of our sales come from grains, bread, pasta, and savory cakes," he explains. At La Ginestra, everything works in tandem, with one element supporting the other. The collective is currently working on building a larger kitchen to produce more food products and help finance other parts of the farm.

Despite the daily financial challenges of operating an employee-owned-and-managed business, Matteo never forgets that turning a profit was never the motivation behind the founding of La Ginestra. For the collective, it has always been about rescuing the land. "If you think that at the end of the year, you need to have a surplus, then that becomes difficult, right? But instead, if you think about just doing what's best for your environment, then it's much simpler. It's more about letting things happen than forcing them with human and scientific power," says Matteo. "It's just a different way of thinking."

5

6

5. Chef Cinzia kneads the dough to make tagliatelle.

6. Fresh-cut tagliatelle.

7. Chef Cinzia made so much tagliatelle that she needs help carrying the pot over to the dining table set outside the *agriturismo*.

7

TAGLIATELLE WITH ZUCCHINI AND GORGONZOLA

SERVES 4

La Ginestra is, in many ways, its own ecosystem—a one-stop shop, if you will. They produce their own wine, harvest honey from their own beehives, cultivate various grains that they transform into flours, breads, and fresh pasta. They even grow their own vegetables, like the zucchini Chef Cinzia used for this recipe, which were abundant during our visit in June 2022. "Fresh handmade pasta is something Cinzia really loves making . . . and with our own raw materials, everything feels extra magical," says Matteo. This recipe serves as a testament to the abundance of the land on which La Ginestra sits.

INGREDIENTS

Special equipment: Pasta roller

Tagliatelle
2¼ cups semi-wholegrain rye flour
2¼ cups semi-wholegrain spelt flour
4 large eggs
Pinch of salt
Semolina flour, for dusting

Sauce
½ cup extra-virgin olive oil
1 cup cubed zucchini
1 clove garlic, finely chopped
1 bunch parsley, chopped
Salt and black pepper
1 large white onion, finely chopped
⅓ cup dry white wine
½ cup béchamel (store-bought or homemade)
½ cup crumbled sweet gorgonzola

INSTRUCTIONS

1. **For the tagliatelle:** Pour both flours onto a clean surface. With your hands, carefully shape the flour into a well and crack the eggs into the center. Add a pinch of salt. Using a fork, slowly incorporate the flour into the egg, beating gently until a shaggy dough begins to form. Knead the dough by hand until the consistency becomes more or less regular. Wrap the dough in plastic wrap and let rest for at least 1 hour and up to 4 hours.

2. To roll out and shape the pasta dough, it is always best to work in batches to avoid the pasta sheets drying. Set up the pasta roller to the widest possible setting. Cut the dough into 4, carefully wrapping the remaining 3 pieces so they don't dry out. Flatten 1 piece of dough with your hands or with a rolling pin to about ⅓-inch thick, then carefully feed it through the roller. Roll it on the same setting once more. Continue rolling the dough through the machine, reducing the settings by one notch each time, until the dough is thin enough that you can begin to see your table through it.

3. Cut the pasta sheet to about 14 inches in length. Dust the sheets with semolina flour and stack them together. Carefully fold them up lengthwise to make them easier to cut. Cut the sheets into ⅓-inch-wide noodles. Unfold the noodles and arrange them on a lightly floured baking sheet and let them dry, tossing every so often, until they feel a bit lighter and stiffer but not brittle, at least 10 minutes. Repeat the rolling, cutting, and drying process with the remaining dough.

4. **For the sauce:** In a medium pan set over medium heat, add 5 tbs of the olive oil, the zucchini, garlic, parsley, and a pinch of salt and pepper. Cook, stirring every once in a while, until the zucchini is golden and soft but not falling apart.

5. In another medium pan set over medium heat, add the remaining 3 tbs olive oil, the onion, and a pinch of salt.

Cook the onions until they turn a light gold color, but not browned, about 5 minutes. Pour in the wine and stir to remove any bits that have stuck to the bottom of the pot. Continue cooking until most of the wine has evaporated, about 2 minutes. Transfer to the pan with the zucchini and turn the heat up to medium. Add the béchamel and stir to combine. Add the gorgonzola and continue cooking until the cheese has melted, about 2 minutes.

6. Bring a large pot of salted water to a boil. Cook the fresh tagliatelle until al dente, 2 to 3 minutes. Strain and return to the pot. Add the zucchini and gorgonzola sauce and toss vigorously to fully coat the tagliatelle. Taste and adjust the seasoning with salt and pepper. Serve immediately.

Lazio

Nestled in the heart of Italy, Lazio is home to the Italian capital of Rome, a city that was once at the helm of the empire responsible for shaping much of Europe's winemaking heritage. Yet, ask anyone to name the most emblematic wine from Lazio and chances are you will be met with a deafening silence. Now, if you ask them the same question about Tuscany, they'll quickly respond with Chianti. Piedmont? Barolo, of course. Lazio? Crickets.

The most famous wine produced in Lazio is Frascati, a white wine made primarily from malvasia and trebbiano grapes grown in the Alban Hills southeast of Rome. Typically light and crisp, with floral and fruity aromas, Frascati used to be a favorite among the nobility of Rome. Today, the wine has largely fallen victim to mass production, causing it to become rather uninteresting. Other notable wines from Lazio include Cesanese del Piglio and Est! Est!! Est!!! di Montefiascone, a white wine with a colorful legend associated with its name. (Legend tells that a scout for a bishop on his way to Rome was tasked with finding inns with the best wines and marking them with the Latin *Est*, or "it is." One Montefiasone wine was so good the scout marked it as *Est! Est!! Est!!!* and the name stuck.)

Despite what its underdevelopment might suggest, the sprawling region of Lazio is actually quite well suited for winemaking. Bordered by the Tyrrhenian Sea to the west, Tuscany to the northwest, Umbria to the north, Marche to the northeast, Abruzzo to the east, and Campania to the southeast, Lazio experiences a Mediterranean climate, with hot, dry summers and mild winters. From the sandy, volcanic soils of the coastal plains to the mineral-rich rocky slopes of the Apennines, the region offers a diverse range of terroirs on which grow a mix of indigenous grapes, including malvasia, trebbiano, cesanese, nero buono, and bellone.

That said, being overlooked comes with a silver lining. Unlike more established wine-growing regions like Tuscany and Piedmont, the price of land in Lazio has remained relatively low and affordable. In recent years, there has been an uptick in the number of young winemakers planting roots throughout the area, which has led to a faint, but growing, buzz surrounding the region.

Much of the recent hype has focused on the volcanic crater lake Lago di Bolsena, where producers like American winemaker Joy Kull at La Villana craft minimal-intervention wines, including a highly drinkable, spirited red wine from the local aleatico grape. A few miles away, former mentors Gianmarco Antonuzi and French-born Clémentine Bouveron at Le Coste, who have been practicing biodynamic winemaking for two decades, have developed a small cult following abroad.

Transplants are not the only ones revitalizing Lazio's winemaking scene. In this section, you will meet Daniele and Pierluca Proietti, the cousins behind Abbia Nòva in their native Piglio, who are dedicated to elevating cesanese with single-parcel bottling. Created by close friend Salvatore Tassa, chef and owner of the Michelin-starred Colline Ciociare, the deceptively simple recipe they shared with us mirrors their winemaking ambitions by bringing local ingredients to new heights.

Abbia Nòva

PIERLUCA & DANIELE PROIETTI

Before committing to a life of winemaking and agriculture, Pierluca Proietti, one half of the cousin duo behind Abbia Nòva, studied philosophy and played indie rock music. Perhaps that's why, during a lengthy lunch at Nù Trattoria, sister restaurant to the Michelin-starred Colline Ciociare, helmed by his friend, chef Salvatore Tassa, the winemaker eagerly draws parallels between wine and music. "Natural wine is like making analog music, and conventional agriculture is similar to digital transformation, like using autotune," muses Pierluca. "In an old-school recording studio, the process is about art, while in a new-style studio, 90 percent of it is technical."

Comparing natural wine to music is nothing new; it is essentially the foundation of *Noble Rot* magazine, a quarterly publication featuring countless thoughtful and poetic analogies. In *The Noble Rot Book: Wine from Another Galaxy* founders Dan Keeling and Marc Andrew liken the natural-wine scene they encountered in Parisian bistros to the early days of indie record labels, describing it as "an authentic culture at odds with the emerging pop-dominated middle ground."

While the jury is still out on whether talking about natural wine and music is still cool or simply cliché, Pierluca's comparison continues to ring true. In the studio or in the cellar, just about anything can be fixed in post. With the right tools, you can make David McMillan sing like Céline Dion or make a wine from California taste like it came from Burgundy. But as Pierluca illustrates, to create something truly special without relying on technology, you have to master the skills and do the necessary work upfront—just like he and his cousin, Daniele Proietti did.

Growing up in Piglio, the rural commune just east of Rome where they now run Abbia Nòva, the cousins were immersed in the worlds of wine and agriculture from a very young age. Pierluca's and Daniele's mothers worked for the local wine cooperative, while Pierluca's father was a farmer interested in natural styles of agriculture. "During the eighties, my father's hobby was to buy small vineyards and plant vines," recalls Pierluca. "It became more than a hobby when he realized he had twenty hectares of land with olive trees and vineyards."

After graduating with a degree in philosophy, Pierluca sought a career path that would connect philosophy and agriculture. Wine, steeped in history and central to many philosophical debates, seemed like a natural choice. Before making the leap, the cousins honed their agricultural skills by exploring the region's history and various approaches, such as biodynamic agriculture, the Natural Farming method developed by Japanese farmer Masanobu Fukuoka, and other homeopathic approaches.

Finally, in 2013, they took over seven hectares of vineyards and land belonging to their family. Their research led them to replace

1

2

copper and sulfur treatments in the vineyard with homemade natural-resistance preparations similar to those used by older farmers in the area. Borrowing from indie music's antiestablishment traditions, the cousins chose to champion ancient varietals native to Lazio, such as cesanese, passerina, bellone, ottonese, and nostrano, instead of cultivating popular international grapes.

Cesanese, with its 500-year-old history deeply rooted in the region, generally yields wines with deeper tones, sizeable tannins, and layers of leather and spice. At Abbia Nòva, the cousins produce a fresh-leaning, broad cesanese cuvée as well as more serious, single-parcel bottlings that express Lazio's underappreciated volcanic terroir. Using passerina, the winemakers craft a bright and vibrant white wine that carries a touch of waxiness in its texture.

After lunch, the duo takes us to their cellar, a rustic structure perched atop a hill. To explain the core of their winemaking philosophy, Pierluca uses another musical analogy, likening the fermentation process to a group of musicians jamming on stage. "You have to know the theory to improvise. Every show will be a little different, but you will learn more each time," he says. "That's why we don't commit to a single method in the vineyard or the cellar." If Abbia Nòva were a band, their discography would feature an array of classical genres, each corresponding to the winemakers' never-ending experiments, such as a one-off bottling of a carbonic macerated cesanese or one of their most ambitious projects to date: high-altitude winemaking.

The cousins have recently started buying and planting vineyards located over 3,200 feet above sea level. In a few years, they hope to expand their existing production to twelve hectares of vines, which would include five hectares of high-altitude vineyards. Growing grapes at high altitude will allow them to experience the effects of a cooler climate on their viticulture, and the grapes will benefit from a different soil composition than the volcanic deposits below. "When you go up the mountain, you will find a lot of rocks, like limestone, which provides grapes with different attributes," Pierluca says. Abbia Nòva has entered its liquid-rock era.

1. Winemaker Pierluca Proiettio.

2. Cousin winemakers Pierluca and Daniele Proietti enjoy lunch at chef Salvatore Tassa's Nù Trattoria, perched in the hills of Acuto.

BAKED PORCINI AND FIG SALAD

SERVES 4

Instead of cooking for us at home, cousins Daniele and Pierluca decided to share one of their yearly culinary traditions with us by visiting chef Salvatore Tassa's Nù Trattoria, located downstairs from his Michelin-starred restaurant, Colline Ciociare, in Acuto. "We come here every year to talk to him about the new vintage," says Pierluca. "His cooking inspires us to forget about theory and to instead focus on keeping our roots firmly planted in our soil, in our history. That's what we try to do with our wine." During our visit, we watched Salvatore effortlessly whip up six portions while juggling another three separate dishes on the stove. Combining the rich earthiness of porcini mushrooms with the sweet, jammy notes of fresh figs, this baked salad comes together in less than 30 minutes and makes quite the first impression, even if you're not planning a multi-course affair.

INGREDIENTS

- 4 medium to large porcini mushrooms (or 8 small)
- 2 tbs plus 2 tsp extra-virgin olive oil
- Salt
- 4 vine leaves, or 4 Swiss chard leaves, or store bought grape leaves in jars
- 4 figs, quartered
- 2 tsp cherry syrup or pomegranate molasses
- 1 tsp fennel seed

INSTRUCTIONS

1. Preheat the oven to 400°F.

2. In a medium bowl, toss the mushrooms with the 2 tbs olive oil and 1 tsp salt. Line 4 small ceramic baking dishes with vine leaves. Distribute the porcini mushrooms and figs in the leaves. Drizzle with cherry syrup and the remaining 2 tsp olive oil. Sprinkle with fennel seeds. Bake for about 18 minutes, until the mushrooms are tender but not mushy. Sprinkle with salt before serving.

Sicily

Few places are as exciting as Sicily. From the fiery peaks of Mount Etna to the azure waves of the Mediterranean Sea crashing against the island's rocky cliffs, the region is characterized by a wildness that countless have tried but, ultimately, failed to tame.

Standing at the crossroads of the Mediterranean Sea, between the eastern coast of Italy and the northern coast of Africa, the region of Sicily is surrounded by several neighboring islands: the Aeolian Islands to the north, the Aegadian Islands to the west, and the windswept Pantelleria off the coast of Tunisia. This strategic position has made it a coveted prize throughout history, leading to countless conquests and invasions by various civilizations, from the Phoenicians to the Greeks, Carthaginians, Romans, Vandals, Byzantines, Arabs, Normans, Spanish, French, and British. Despite its incorporation into the newly unified Italy in 1860, Sicily has retained its fiercely independent spirit. By 1946, it had ceased to be entirely submissive to Rome, emerging as one of Italy's five semiautonomous regions and governed by its own distinct laws and customs.

The region's winemaking history is a rich tapestry woven together by the various civilizations that have inhabited the island over millennia. The Greeks are credited with laying the foundations of viticulture and winemaking in the region, while the Romans further developed Sicily's vineyards, exporting its wines across

the empire. Subsequent Arab rule introduced new grape varietals such as moscato, zibibbo (or muscat d'Alexandrie), and albanello. However, it wasn't until the Spanish Bourbon dynasty took control of the region that Sicily's winemaking industry truly flourished, with the invention of marsala, a fortified wine crafted in both sweet and dry styles. While it became synonymous with Sicily as the region's biggest export, marsala never attained the prestigious status of other Italian wines like Barolo.

This began to change in recent years, with winemakers in the northwestern region crafting high-quality, terroir-expressive marsala using traditional noninterventionist methods. As it happens, this shift toward natural winemaking with a focus on terroir wasn't an isolated incident. In fact, over the past few decades, Sicily has become a bona fide playground for natural winemakers who, unlike occupying forces of yesteryear, have understood that they're better off letting the land speak for itself.

The heart of Sicily's natural winemaking renaissance beats to the rhythm of Mount Etna, Europe's tallest and most active volcano. Made up of a mineral-rich mix of ash, lava, and pumice, Etna's slopes are dotted with vineyards, their altitudes ranging between 400 to 1,000 meters above sea level. Among them are vines tended by Sicilian-born legend Salvo Foti and natural-wine superstar Frank Cornelissen, with local varietals like nerello mascalese, carricante, and catarratto.

In the southeastern part of the island, many natural wineries have also emerged, led by vocal natural-wine advocate Arianna Occhipinti, whose work has sparked a frappato revival in the region.

In this chapter, you'll experience Sicily through the perspectives of three winemakers representing some of its most dynamic regions. Our journey begins with the dragon of Mount Etna, Frank Cornelissen, whose influence on the natural-wine world has been nothing short of profound. Next, we'll venture near the town of Noto to explore the family-run winery Cantina Marilina. Finally, we'll cross the sea to meet natural-wine sensation Gabrio Bini at Azienda Agricola Serragghia, whose arrow labels have all heads turning toward Pantelleria. Each recipe that follows reflects the winemakers' personal histories and connections to Sicily's rugged landscape.

Azienda Agricola Frank Cornelissen

FRANK CORNELISSEN

It's a scorching 100 degrees Fahrenheit (ca. 38 degree Celsius) on Mount Etna, and winemaker Frank Cornelissen is racing around every twist and turn of the Sicilian volcano's cliff-hugging roads. Steph and Xavier, unusually silent in the back seat, cling to each other nervously with their eyes closed. "Etna has some of the best roads in the country," Frank remarks with a grin as he shifts gears. Despite his love for speed, Frank's journey to becoming a natural wine mainstay has been remarkably measured.

Born and raised in Belgium, Frank's passion for food and wine blossomed early, influenced by his father, who he describes as an avid enthusiast and amateur collector of classical wines. "Well, he wasn't exactly collecting—more like we'd drink everything when it hit the perfect age," he chuckles.

After a stint working for an Italian wine importer, where he grew wary of limiting his wine knowledge, Frank transitioned to overseeing

1. Mount Etna's landscape and vegetation are lush, with the mouth of the volcano always looming in the distance.

2. Small one-lane roads wind their way up Mount Etna.

3. Winemaker Frank Cornelissen is in the midst of transforming old, run-down buildings in Solicchiata into his new home and winery.

3

the cellars of affluent private clients, tasting and sourcing wine on their behalf. This move not only deepened his grasp of classical wines but also broadened his palate, bringing him into contact with smaller producers like La Biancara, the Veneto winery led by natural-wine pioneer Angiolino Maule. Captivated by Maule's living wines, Frank ventured deeper into the world of natural wine. Soon, he started making regular trips to Paris, where he immersed himself in the city's burgeoning natural-wine community.

By the late 1990s, the idea of venturing into winemaking had begun to rev up in Frank's mind. But it wasn't until the year 2000, during a trip to Sicily, that the dream of Mount Etna unexpectedly came crashing into his life after he blind-tasted a bottle with a friend. "Nobody at the table could believe the wine was from Etna," Frank recalls. "It was incredibly profound."

At that time, the winemaking scene on Mount Etna was quite different from what it is today. While producers like Marco de Grazia of Tenuta delle Terre Nere and Andrea Franchetti of Passopisciaro were beginning to explore the terroir's potential, most of the region's industry was dominated by cooperatives focused on producing bulk wine. Eager to meet the winemakers behind the bottle that had deeply moved him, Frank set off for Etna. "I didn't find the winery, but as I drove around the valley, I felt like, *boom*, this is it," he says.

In 2001, still enthralled by Mount Etna's rugged beauty, Frank established his winery on a small plot of land on the volcano's northern slopes. From the outset, he believed that the region's unique terroir, defined by rich, phylloxera-resistant volcanic soils and ancient ungrafted vines, could rival the world's top wine regions. Guided by a vision to create wines that truly reflected Etna, Frank avoided chemical treatments in the vineyard. In the cellar, he embraced spontaneous fermentations, experimented with co-fermentations, and explored skin-contact macerations for white wines, all without added sulfites or filtration.

"I wanted to create the greatest terroir wines from Etna and not copy Burgundy or Barolo," he explains. To achieve this, he broke down his production into two main categories: The first included entry-level estate wines such as Susucaru rosato, Susucaru rosso (formerly Contadino), MunJebel Bianco, and MunJebel Rosso, produced with grapes sourced from various vineyard sites. In the second category, Frank focused on single-vineyard bottlings to deepen

his exploration of Etna's terroir and highlight each site's unique characteristics. His single-vineyard MunJebel cuvées are identified by letters corresponding to distinct vineyard locations like MC (Monte Colla), VA (Vigne Alta), and PU (Puntalazzo). Meanwhile, Magma, his most expensive wine, is produced using the finest nerello mascalese grapes from his Barbabecchi vineyard.

Frank parks the car on the side of the road. Still a bit dizzy from the drive, we trail behind the winemaker as he heads across the street toward the base of Barbabecchi. Perched at around 3,000 feet above sea level, the lush vineyard unfolds with terraced rows of ancient vines interwoven with vibrant purple and yellow flowers embedded in Etna's dark volcanic soil. As we reach the top to take in the sweeping views of the valley below, we are overcome with the familiar feeling that we've stumbled upon something special.

It's the same feeling many of us experienced when we encountered Frank's early wines. The first vintages of Susucaru rosato, in particular, felt like a journey into uncharted territory. Unconventional yet vibrant, the wine was bursting with fresh fruit and characterized by a distinctive minerality and the absence of added sulfites.

Even the packaging felt like a revolution in and of itself: a clear bottle with a transparent printed-on label that allowed the wine's cherry-ring-pop color and cloudy appearance to shine through. "In the late 1990s and early 2000s, it was all about big, super-concentrated wines. I wanted people to see the color of my wines to show that not everything had to be big and thick," says Frank, about selling red wine in a clear bottle, a decision that ended up changing the face of natural-wine forever.

Following the widespread success of his entry-level wines and notable media appearances (including a tasting on Vice's Munchies channel with rapper Action Bronson and our friend, the late wine director Justin Chearno), attention

5

4. Farming the vines on Mount Etna, Frank and his team have spent almost as much time repairing the vineyard walls that hold the terraced parcels of nerello mascalese.

5. Frank smiling inside his new house, which is still under construction.

shifted to Frank's single-vineyard expressions. His terroir-focused approach inspired other producers in the region to follow suit. This movement culminated in the establishment of contrada on Etna (similar to crus in Burgundy), proving that Frank was right in believing that Etna was a premier wine-producing region.

Later that day, Frank drives us to his new house and winery, still under construction. From the front, it looks like any other building on Etna—old and weathered. But as the car pulls around to the back of the house, the scene transforms. There, revealed in full, is a striking brutalist structure made of concrete that looks like a Bond villain lair if it were designed by Japanese architect Tadao Ando. While this marks a significant departure from the winemaker's modest beginnings some twenty years ago, it's not just the winery that has undergone a massive transformation—so have Frank's wines.

Now producing around 140,000 bottles annually, Frank is quick to admit that his early wines, while instrumental in Etna's winemaking renaissance, were wildly inconsistent. In recent years, the winemaker has adjusted his approach to sulfites, acknowledging the benefits of using minimal amounts to ensure stability and longevity, particularly for wines intended for ageing or wider distribution. "I think my wines today rank among the absolute best in the world, but to get there, I had to fumble and push the boundaries," says Frank. "And you know, that takes time."

6

7

6. Lunch at Cave Ox, the beating heart of Mount Etna, where the region's best wines are on offer.

7. Pallets of wine heading for Quebec.

TEMPURA ARTICHOKE HEARTS

SERVES 2–4

"Artichokes are not meant to be served with wine, in general, but if you have really great wines—wines with body, strength and profoundness—it works," says Frank. "Tempura sort of pulls out the sweetness from the artichoke, and mellows it." This simple fried artichoke recipe is a nod to Frank's wife, Aki, and her Japanese heritage, while also recalling the fried artichoke you can find in Sicily's famous food markets. Pro tip: pair your tempura with Gabrio Bini's caper condiment (page 244).

INGREDIENTS

Special equipment: Frying thermometer

Juice of 1 lemon
12 small artichokes
1 cup wholewheat flour
6 cups extra-virgin olive oil
Salt and black pepper

INSTRUCTIONS

1. In a large bowl, add 3 cups of cold water and the lemon juice. Peel and quarter the artichokes, removing the hairy choke with a spoon. Place in the bowl to prevent them from browning.

2. In a medium mixing bowl, combine 1½ cups cold water and the flour. Whisk until smooth, ensuring the batter has a pancake-like consistency.

3. In a deep-frying pan or small Dutch oven, heat the olive oil until it reaches a temperature of 270°F, using a frying thermometer to monitor the temperature.

4. Remove the artichokes from the water and dry thoroughly with paper towels. Working in small batches (about 4 pieces at a time), dip the artichokes in the batter, ensuring they are evenly coated, then carefully drop them into the hot oil. Use tongs to prevent sticking and ensure even frying. Flip and turn occasionally to cook both sides. Fry until they are golden brown, approximately 2 minutes per batch.

5. Remove the artichokes from the oil and place them on paper towels to drain excess oil. Sprinkle the fried artichokes with salt and pepper. Repeat the process in batches until all the artichokes have been fried. Serve the artichokes while they are still warm.

Cantina Marilina

MARILINA PATERNÒ

"Stop it," says Marilina Paternò, laughing as she gently swats her father's hand away, which, only moments ago, was lovingly petting her head. Now, with both hands resting on his daughter's shoulders, Angelo Paternò smiles proudly as he watches her discuss the nuances of the previous year's vintage with Zev.

In her thirties, Marilina now runs the winery founded by her father, while parenting two young children, the impossibly cute Cecilia and Rosario. But in that moment, with Angelo by her side, it's hard not to picture the winemaker as a child, running between barrels of wine, chasing her father around the cellar with her sister, Federica, in tow. "As children, during harvest, we played with the stems and followed the grapes through all the stages, tasting them often," recalls Marilina. "And my father would let me drink the must."

Throughout Marilina's childhood, the Paternò family frequently moved around Sicily due to Angelo's work as the winemaker and technical director for large-scale Sicilian wineries, including Cantine Settesoli and Duca di Salaparuta. Deep down, Angelo dreamed of operating a family-run winery that he could eventually pass on to his children. In 2001, after saving enough money, he purchased sixty hectares of land on a hill formerly known as Poggio dei Fossi in the province of Siracusa, near Pachino, a town known for its sweet Datterini tomatoes. Believing in the interconnectedness of the ecosystem's various elements and the importance of giving back to nature instead of solely taking, Angelo prioritized enhancing biodiversity and soil health through polyculture. He dedicated thirty-five hectares of the land to growing a variety of grapes—nero d'Avola, grecanico, muscat blanc, moscato giallo, insolia, merlot, tannat, viognier, and chardonnay—while devoting the rest to the cultivation of grains and fruits.

It's possible the presence of Marilina's kids or the winery's children's-book-inspired labels played a trick on our minds during our visit, but in many ways, the story of Marilina and Angelo conjured the Disney classic *The Lion King*. Marilina escaping her dad's embrace like Simba had with his mother. The young girl playing around the cellar, too young to fully understand yet already absorbing her father's teachings about a world that will soon be hers. Even Angelo's philosophy seemed to echo Mufasa's Circle of Life speech: "Everything you see exists together in a delicate balance. When we die, our bodies become the grass, and the antelope eat the grass. And so we are all connected in the great Circle of Life."

The next day, Angelo's commitment to biodiversity becomes even more evident when he

1. (Left) Marilina Paternò carries her son, Rosario, through the cellar, past pallets of empty bottles waiting to be filled.

2. Winemaker Marilina Paternò.

takes us on a car ride to show us a small plot of old sapling vines of white moscato. Formerly called muscatedda, the vines yield small, loose bunches plump with amber-colored grapes. Perhaps the most surprising aspect isn't the bush-like shape of the vines but rather the ground, which shines bright orange with ripe apricots fallen from the many fruit trees scattered among a sea of vines and towering cacti. "In the grapes of this moscato, you can feel all the aromas of the trees planted with it—apricots, figs, citrus fruits, medlars," says Marilina.

Back at the house, Marilina's mother, Lina, shows us around the kitchen while regaling us with stories of her time as a traveling chef. (As a result of one of her gigs, her face is even featured on popular sauce packets across Japan.) The matriarch now oversees the production of jams, olive oil, and homemade pasta at Cantina Marilina. Angelo quietly pops his head into the kitchen, ready to show us around the cellar.

Completed in 2009, the cellar was always part of Angelo and Marilina's vision for the winery. They envisioned a large structure adjacent to the house to make and store wines that expressed their Sicilian heritage. They also aimed to create something that could be passed down to the next generation, continuing the family legacy started by Angelo. Shortly after the cellar was built, Angelo handed over the reins to Marilina and Federica. Although Federica has since taken a different path, Marilina remains in charge, accompanied by her father.

3

4

3. Marilina's daughter, Cecilia, and some locals enjoy time in the yard.

4. Winemaker and patriarch Angelo Paternò has been making wines in Sicily for decades.

5. Fresh focaccia dough ready to be baked.

6. Matriarch Lina Paternò prepares Pane Fritto con L'Uovo.

5

6

"The relationship between my father and me is one of the strongest in the world," says Marilina. "We are accomplices and support each other. I'm lucky to have him next to me. He has always welcomed my proposals, and we always strive to balance history and experience with a vision for the future."

Angelo leads us toward the cellar, followed closely by Marilina, who is carrying a feverish Rosario in her arms, and Cecilia, who, in contrast, is bursting with energy. Once inside, we are met with towering concrete tanks in which most of their wines ferment and age, including an earthy, broad-shouldered nero d'Avola, whose tannins are somewhat softened by the ageing vessel. In another room, we find large oak barrels filled with, among other wines, the domaine's Cécile cuvée. Named after Marilina's daughter, Cécile (the French form of Cecilia) is a structured, creamsicle-hued, skin-macerated moscato aged for almost three years (twenty-eight months in neutral oak, followed by six months in bottle). On his way out of the room, Angelo stops talking mid-sentence and turns around to chase after Cecilia who, until now, had been hiding between barrels, much like her mother did at her age. It's the circle of life.

ZUCCHINI LEAF SOUP

SERVES 4-6

Tenerumi soup is a traditional Sicilian dish that embodies the region's peasant cooking roots. Making use of every edible part of the plant, this hearty soup features the tender shoots and leaves of the zucchini plant (tenerumi), prized for their delicate texture and subtle flavor. "Because tenerumi sounds a lot like tenerezza, the Italian word for tenderness, it always reminds me of my grandmother, who used to make this recipe for us in the summer," says Marilina.

INGREDIENTS

- 1 lb young zucchini shoots and tendrils, roughly chopped
- ¼ lb Datterini, cherry, or grape tomatoes, halved
- 1 white onion, thinly sliced
- 3 medium yellow potatoes, peeled and cut into dice-size cubes
- Salt and black pepper
- 1 lb spaghetti, broken into two-inches pieces
- Extra-virgin olive oil, for serving

INSTRUCTIONS

1. In a large pot, add 8 cups of water and bring to a boil over high heat. Add the zucchini shoots and tendrils, tomatoes, and onion. Reduce the heat to low and simmer for 10 minutes. Add the potatoes, 1 tsp salt, and 1 tsp pepper and cook until the potatoes are fork-tender but not mushy, about 10 minutes. Add the spaghetti and cook until al dente, about 8 minutes. You can add water sparingly, as if cooking a risotto—the final result should be somewhere between a noodle soup and a pasta dish. Remove from the heat, taste the broth, and adjust the seasoning with salt and pepper. Divide the soup among bowls, drizzle with olive oil, and serve immediately.

FRIED BREAD WITH EGGS

SERVES 6–8

Known as "pane fritto con l'uovo" in Italian, this simple dish embodies Sicily's peasant cooking traditions. Historically prepared during the harvest season, it served as a valuable source of protein for farmers working long hours in the field. Since money was often tight, this recipe enabled them to repurpose stale bread by soaking it in eggs until it softened up again before frying. Marilina's version can easily be adapted to your liking by swapping out the basil for any other savory herb of your choosing.

INGREDIENTS

10 large eggs
Salt and black pepper
20 fresh basil leaves, thinly sliced
Extra-virgin olive oil
1 loaf bread, sliced

INSTRUCTIONS

1. In a large bowl, beat the eggs. Add a pinch of salt and pepper, and the basil.

2. In a large frying pan, heat 2 tbs olive oil over medium-high heat. Working in batches of 1 to 3 slices, depending on the size of your pan, dip the bread slices into the beaten egg mixture, making sure each slice absorbs as much liquid as possible.

3. Add the dipped bread to the hot pan and fry on each side until golden, about 2 minutes per side. Repeat the process until all the bread has been fried. Serve immediately while the fried bread is still hot.

Azienda Agricola Serragghia

GABRIO, GENEVIÈVE & GIOTTO BINI

Driving around Pantelleria feels like a surrealist dream. Forged by ancient volcanic fires, the island rises out of the Mediterranean Sea, somewhere between the coasts of Italy and Tunisia. Winding roads, bordered by obsidian-stone walls, meander through the countryside, from the imposing Montagna Grande to the healing sulphuric waters of Lago di Venera, leading to secluded coves and grottos where the water shimmers in shades of turquoise and emerald. Even the air on Pantelleria, a heady mix of salt and the fragrant aromas of wild herbs and flowering caper plants, carries with it a sense of exuberant beauty that veers on the fantastical.

The island is a fitting backdrop for an exuberant man like Gabrio Bini, the eccentric architect-turned-winemaker who so beautifully captures Pantelleria's boisterous mystique inside his signature arrow-clad bottles. When we meet him at his house, tucked in the hilly heartland, the winemaker is on the phone with his wife, Geneviève. Standing in front of his son Giotto's *dammuso*, a traditional stone house known for its distinctive white-domed roof, Gabrio's white hair and chartreuse-green silk shirt are swaying in the wind. He waves at us, his wide smile framed by his famous mustache, which makes him look like natural-wine's answer to Salvador Dalí.

Gabrio Bini was born in Florence to artist parents. His mother was a seamstress and his father a classical dancer. When Gabrio's father landed a job dancing at the famed Teatro alla Scala, the family relocated to Milan, where

3

Gabrio studied architecture. After graduation, he began working on a variety of local and international projects, anywhere from Bulgaria to Japan. He even collaborated with his brothers Nino and Stefano on designing futuristic showrooms for the Italian-born French fashion designer Pierre Cardin. During those days, Gabrio spent a lot of time in Paris, where he eventually met Geneviève, a French creative director working in advertising. The two would go on to marry and split their time between Paris and Milan.

In 1994, after a few visits to Pantelleria on vacation with their son, Giotto, the couple decided to purchase a holiday home on the island. The house they found was tucked in the hills and surrounded by caper plants, as well as one hectare of vines. Despite being an avid wine drinker and admirer of Pierre Overnoy's work, Gabrio had never considered becoming a winemaker himself. That was until his friend Attilio Scienza, a viticulture professor at the agricultural school in Milan,

4

1. Winemaker Gabrio Bini leads us into the hills of Pantelleria.

2. The Binis bury their amphoras in the ground to regulate the temperature and protect the wines from the island's scorching heat.

3. Horses Flora and Uma Kuda enjoy some hay in the terraced vineyards above the winery.

4. Gabrio and Geneviève's son, winemaker Giotto Bini.

pointed out that the architect was in possession of a pristine vineyard sitting on fantastic volcanic terroir. It would still take another ten years for Gabrio to make his first wines.

So if we call Pantelleria a surrealist dream, the Gabrio Bini estate is a Dalí painting come to life. Purple caper flowers sprout from every possible crack on the stone-paved outdoor pathways. His house—three *magazzini* (traditional stone warehouses) joined together—appears to be growing out of a bed of cacti and generous bougainvilleas. In lieu of a back door, a beaded crystal curtain acts as a trompe l'oeil waterfall. Outside, an imposing dining table designed by Gabrio features a blue Brazilian marble top that imitates the sky, and a colorful, mobile footrest that emits a musical, gong-like sound as it moves. A few steps further, a gigantic clay amphora is perched, overlooking the terraced vineyards and the sea below. In the distance, Uma Uda, Gabrio's miniature horse, can be seen playing with Flora, her regular-size counterpart, who helps the Bini family with harvest.

"I make wine like an architect," says Gabrio, when asked why it took him so long to make his first vintage. He started by hiring an agronomist to analyze the soil's composition and biology. Then, he spent years researching ancient winemaking techniques and materials, the exact same way an architect would before deciding on a particular tile or marble for a project. He traveled to Georgia, Spain, and across Italy to learn about clay amphoras, eventually preferring the Spanish-made vessels. "It would have been much easier to get amphoras made in Sicily, but the clay used here is not great for winemaking," he explains.

Gabrio leads us behind his house to an open-air stone structure adorned with miniature amphoras. "Now I buy amphoras from an Italian company called TAVA in Trento, which makes magnificent amphoras with the guidance of my friend Attilio Scienza," says the winemaker. Inside, dozens of empty Spanish and northern Italian clay amphoras peek from underneath the ground. In a few months, they will be filled with this year's vintage.

While he often jokes that most people can finish a few college degrees in the time it took him to make his first bottle of wine, Gabrio felt like he had to lay a solid foundation in order to make wine the way he wanted to—naturally. "It's not a philosophy, it's a process," he says of his work as a winemaker. Studying and considering every variable carefully, from the soil to

5.

5. Geneviève Bini with her dogs, Baik Baik and Onda, outside their friend's restaurant Rifugio Firiçiakki, tucked in the hills of Pantelleria.

6. Traditional Pantelleria *dammuso* houses are characterized by their distinctive white-domed roofs.

7. Blooming agave plants tower all over the island.

viticulture practices and fermentation vessels, allows him to let the grapes express the island's terroir without having to worry too much.

Gabrio's wines are a true expression of the man and the island that birthed them: fragrant, exuberant, and adventurous. Zibibbo (a white grape known as muscat d'Alexandrie that grows around the island) injects electricity into Gabrio's wines, before exploding into an aromatic bouquet reminiscent of potpourri. Generally speaking, the winery's white wines, which are long-macerated in amphora, are textured and perfumed. The domaine's flagship co-fermented red and white wine, Fanino, blends the juiciness of pignatello with the bright aromatics of catarratto.

The first vintage was small—about 700 bottles were released under the name Azienda Agricola Serragghia, all of which were purchased by a friend who distributed natural wines in Italy. Despite having purchased other surrounding vineyards since 2005, Gabrio's production remains small, with yields that hover around 40 hectoliters per hectare. Comparatively, other winemakers on the island achieve yields closer to 100 hectoliters

7

per hectare. With that in mind, the winemaker understood early on that for him to sustainably make wine without having to further expand his production (thus overexerting himself as well as the land), he would have to create high-quality wines that would fall into a higher price range.

"The thing with wine is that you don't simply make it and drink it, you also have to give it an image," says Gabrio. With Geneviève's background in advertising and his background in design and architecture, it makes sense that the couple ended up creating one of the most iconic natural-wine labels of all time: the arrow. Originally created as a light fixture for one of Geneviève's jobs, which now hangs in the couple's house in Palermo, the arrow now comes in an array of colors corresponding to different cuvées.

Since his first vintage almost twenty years ago, the mustachioed Milanese architect-turned-winemaker has become a darling of both the natural-wine and fashion communities. His wines can be spotted all over the world, with Bini fans posting photos on Instagram with the famous arrow pointed directly at their heads. The winemaker's popularity has also brought about clothing collaborations and modeling campaigns with brands like Our Legacy and A.P.C.

More recently, Gabrio started building a winemaking facility for him and Giotto to craft high-quality wines instead of continuing to use a space shared with other winemakers. The financial pressure linked to the construction of the new winery has pushed Gabrio to come up with creative ways to generate revenue, short of raising

6

prices of existing cuvées or resorting to producing lesser-quality wines. Instead, the winemaker has taken a page out of the fashion industry's playbook by creating expensive, limited-edition cuvées that appeal to collectors.

Later that night, as we gather around the table, Gabrio pulls out an unmarked bottle from his bag. Curious, we watch as he meticulously applies a fresh sticker to the bottle. He turns it around to reveal the label: a golden arrow adorned with the phrase *Parisien par Amour* (Parisian by Love). With only fifty-two bottles made and retailing at about $1,500, the wine is a blend of Jura varietals grown on Pantelleria from clippings gifted by natural-wine legends. "The poulsard was given to me by my friend Stéphane Tissot, and the savagnin by Pierre Overnoy, who for me, is the pope of wine," says Gabrio. Not only is the wine phenomenal, but Parisien par Amour feels, above all, like a surreal retrospective of Gabrio's life in bottle form: a love letter to his Parisian wife, Geneviève; a nod to his natural-wine heroes; and in true Bini fashion, a stroke of branding genius.

8

8. Gabrio listens to what the amphoras have to say.

9. (Right) Gabrio Bini opens a magnum of zibibbo inside his kitchen, with an arrow-clad wine box in the background.

PANELLE WITH SPICY CAPER CONDIMENT

SERVES 4

If you don't know what a caper plant looks like before visiting Pantelleria, you'll certainly become familiar with it there. While cities often see invasive weeds grow through cracks in the pavement, in Pantelleria, it's caper plants' glossy green leaves and showy purple flowers that sprout seemingly everywhere. Prized around the world, the island's capers are known for their mineral and tangy-savory flavor profile, imparted by the island's volcanic soil. The Bini family even produces the sought-after Serragghia di Pantelleria capers showered in French Fleur de sel de Guérande salt, a nod to Geneviève's home country. The caper condiment recipe below yields extra, which we suggest using on fresh fish crudo, cooked fish, and even chicken.

As for the crispy chickpea flour fritters known as panelle, they are a traditional Sicilian street food with origins that can be traced back to the Arab influence in the region during the Middle Ages. Gabrio served these as an antipasto, hot and fresh from the fryer, accompanied by a few lemon wedges and a dollop of spicy caper condiment.

INGREDIENTS

Spicy Caper Condiment (makes about 2 cups)
- ½ cup salt-packed capers
- ½ cup almonds
- ½ cup parsley
- 10 anchovy fillets
- 1 tbs Tabasco sauce
- 1 tsp freshly ground black pepper
- ¼ cup extra-virgin olive oil
- 1 tbs fresh lemon juice

Panelle
- 4⅓ cups chickpea flour
- 4 tbs parsley, chopped
- Salt and black pepper
- 6 cups of neutral oil for frying
- 2 lemons, cut into wedges, for serving

INSTRUCTIONS

1. **For the spicy caper condiment:** Place the capers in a large bowl and cover them with 1 cup cold water. Let the capers rest 8 to 10 hours, changing the water every 2 to 3 hours. Drain the water and rinse the capers before using.

2. In a food processor or a blender, combine the capers with the rest of the ingredients, and pulse until the mixture is homogeneous and fairly smooth. The condiment can be served immediately or stored in an airtight container in the fridge for up to 1 week.

3. **For the panelle:** Add 6 ⅓ cups water to a medium pot set over low heat. Little by little, add the chickpea flour, whisking constantly to avoid clumping, until all the flour has been incorporated. Continue cooking on low, stirring often to avoid sticking, until the dough begins to come off the edge of the pot, 40 to 45 minutes. Add the parsley, 1 tsp salt, and 1 tsp pepper and stir to combine. Transfer the dough to a baking sheet and let it rest for about 4 hours.

4. stir to combine. On a lightly floured surface roll out the dough until it reaches the size of a large baking sheet. Carefully transfer the dough to the baking sheet and press it firmly against the edges. Trim any excess dough and let it rest, covered, for about 4 hours. Add enough frying oil to a shallow pan to reach a depth of ⅓ inch, and set over medium-high heat. The oil is hot enough for frying when a pinch of dough added to the pan sputters.

5. Working in batches, fry the dough until golden brown and crispy. Using tongs or a slotted spoon, transfer the panelle to the prepared baking sheet and sprinkle with salt. Repeat the process in batches until all the panelle have been fried. Serve immediately with a dollop of spicy caper condiment and a few lemon wedges.

Further Readings

Despite the fact that we never designed this book to become a serious wine reference, we do hope you enjoyed getting to know the natural winemakers we've had the pleasure of spending time with over the last few years. If you're looking to deepen your understanding of wine, natural or otherwise, we've compiled a list of our favorite books on the topic.

A Glass of Wine, A Breath of Fresh Air
by Jean-Pierre Frick

Adventures on the Wine Route
by Kermit Lynch

Amber Revolution: How the World Learned to Love Orange Wine
by Simon J. Woolf

Authentic Wine: Toward Natural and Sustainable Winemaking
by Jamie Goode

Bordeaux: A Consumer's Guide to the World's Finest Wines
by Robert M. Parker

Burgundy: A Comprehensive Guide to the Producers, Appellations, and Wines
by Robert M. Parker

The Esthetics of Wine
by Jules Chauvet

Friuli Food and Wine: Frasca Cooking from Northern Italy's Mountains, Vineyards, and Seaside
by Bobby Stuckey, Lachlan Mackinnon-Patterson, and Meredith Erickson

Naked Wine: Letting Grapes Do What Comes Naturally
by Alice Feiring

Natural Wine: An Introduction to Organic and Biodynamic Wines Made Naturally
by Isabelle Legeron

The New French Wine: Redefining the World's Greatest Wine Culture
by Jon Bonné

The Noble Rot Book: Wine from Another Galaxy
by Dan Keeling and Mark Andrew

One Thousand Vines: A New Way to Understand Wine
by Pascaline Lepeltier

The Pentagon: Memoirs on the Agricultural Philosophy Understanding of Vine and Wine
by Rainer Zierock (Disclaimer: Gifted to us by Elisabetta Foradori, this one might be impossible to find)

Poetry Is Growing in Our Garden
by Anders Frederik Steen

The Science of Wine: from Vine to Glass
by Jamie Goode

Vino: The Essential Guide to Real Italian Wine
by Joe Campanale with Joshua David Stein

Wine in Question
by Jules Chauvet

The Wine Snob's Dictionary: An Essential Lexicon of Oenological Knowledge
by David Kamp and David Lynch

The Wines of the Northern Rhône
by John Livingstone-Learmonth

The World of Natural Wine: What It Is, Who Makes It, and Why It Matters
by Aaron Ayscough

Acknowledgments

Thank you to all the winemakers featured in this book for opening your homes and kitchens to us, and for trusting us with sharing your stories and recipes. This book was first and foremost written to honor your passion and generosity, which truly knows no bounds. We are eternally grateful for your friendship, as well as for all the wine. To all the other winemakers, harvesters, restaurateurs, friends, and general bons vivants we met during our travels, thank you for making writing a book fun.

Thank you to Andy Beauchesne for your recipe-testing insights and for allowing us to turn on every oven in yours and David's house during a scorching heatwave. To Robb Jamieson and Juliette Robinot, thank you for your fact-checking assistance, which prevented Steph from losing her mind any further.

Thank you to Emilie Campbell for being our collective best friend, one of the smartest wine people we know, and the kind of mind-reading artist who knows to include Easter eggs in her illustrations without us even having to ask. To our friends at Perron-Roettinger—Willo, Brian, and Veronica—thank you for bringing this book to life. Your designs turned our buffoonery into a beautiful, unique object and for that we are forever grateful.

Thank you to our literary agent Kimberly Witherspoon, and to Maria Whelan, for believing in our vision and never giving up on this book, even when we nearly did. Thank you to our editor, Ellen Nidy, at Rizzoli for immediately understanding what we were trying to say with this odd natural-wine cookbook. To the rest of the team at Rizzoli, thank you for letting us make the kind of book that didn't quite exist before.

Stephanie would like to thank: David, for trusting me with the idea for this book at a time when I didn't have much to show for it. Thanks to Xavier, for being by my side since day one, which now feels like a lifetime of inside jokes ago, or perhaps just one *grosse journée au bureau*. Zev, thank you for always being down—whether it's to join this project before ever meeting me, allowing us to spend time with winemakers you hold dear, or simply for always saying yes to one more drink when I'm not ready to go home. But, above all, thank you for always driving (and sorry I drove your car into a ditch that one time). Thank you to Emilie for being the most supportive and loving wife, and for allowing me to claim the office for over two years. To Rachel, from gossiping at L'Express after wine school to today, thank you for your unwavering friendship. Not a day goes by that I don't miss living in the same city as you. Thank you to Ryan for being the first (!) to make me care about natural wine and its people. To my family, thank you for always being my biggest cheerleaders, even if I don't visit as often as I should. Thank you to everyone at The Four Horsemen for allowing me the time and support to write (and complain) about this book. To Justin, thank you for all the chats and text threads—your wit and bullshit detector inspired some of my favorite bits in this book. I think you would've been proud of us. To all the friends whose calls and texts I've ignored while writing this book, I'm sorry. . . let's catch up over a bottle soon.

David would like to thank: Steph for steering the ship of fools and always being funny. Thank you, Zev, for being a legend. Xavier, I am slowly warming up to you. Thank you to Cassady Sniatowsky for ideas, counsel, friendship, conversation, and clairvoyance. Thanks to Andy Beauchesne for putting up with me and my ideas, I love you. To my lovely children Flynn, Ceçi, Lola, Dylan, I love you very much.

Zev would like to thank: Steph and Xav for all of your hard work, which has made it easy for me to put my name on a book, and for keeping spirits high during our long road trips with your hearty laughter that more often than not sounds like screaming. Even if nobody reads this book, at least I got you as lifelong friends because of it. Thanks to David for having a strangely profound understanding of the human condition and the ability to come up with ideas such as this one. Emilie, thank you for possessing the secret skill of being an incredible illustrator and managing to do it while working two very full-time jobs.

Xavier would like to thank: Steph, as one of my closest friends and someone I've been dreaming of making books with for over a decade, thank you for inviting me on a random press trip to Slovenia and Italy back in 2018 to try to make this book happen. Look at where we are now. Zev, thank you, or whatever… I love you from the bottom of my heart, and I am so grateful that this project brought us together. Thank you for opening up your world and letting us share such special moments with you. David, thank you for believing in Steph and me, always pushing hard for this book to get made. You are a true legend. Thank you for wanting to share stories your way and for doing it well. Thanks to all the winemakers for being such good sports and playing the photo game with me. Despite how annoying it can be to have me direct you for a photo while you're cooking or trying to work, you always made us feel like we were family. To my other great friend, Emilie, from the road trips around Quebec back when we worked together in Montreal to now doodling me in the vines and making me look cute, thank you for everything. Thank you to Janie for always letting me do what I love most. This book is a beautiful love letter to old and new friendships.

Index

Page references in italics denote recipes.

A

Abbia Nòva (winery), 216–219
    Baked Porcini and Fig Salad, *218–219*
acidifiers and deacidifiers, 23
additives in conventional winemaking, 23, 24
almonds
    Panelle with Spicy Caper Condiment, *244–245*
ambient yeast
    in the cellar, 24
    defined, 19
    in the vineyard, 19
amphora (vessel), 17
anchovy
    Panelle with Spicy Caper Condiment, *244–245*
appellation, defined, 17
Apple Mostarda, *204–205*
apricots
    Baking Sheet Pear Tart, *138–139*
artichoke
    Tempura Artichoke Hearts, *228–229*
Auvergne, France, 125–139
    Domaine la Bohème, 126–133
    Tricot, Marie and Vincent, 134–139
Azienda Agricola Dario Prinčič (winery), 175, 176–181
    Rabbit Biechi, *180–181*
Azienda Agricola Foradori (winery), 26, 184–189
    Zucchini Soup with Fresh Cheese, *188–189*
Azienda Agricola Frank Cornelissen (winery), 26, 222–229
    Tempura Artichoke Hearts, *228–229*
Azienda Agricola Serragghia (winery), 238–245
    Panelle with Spicy Caper Condiment, *244–245*

B

bacon
    Boeuf Bourguignon, *104–105*
    Caillettes, *160–161*
    Quiche Lorraine with Wild Mushrooms, *90–91*
Baked Porcini and Fig Salad, *218–219*
Baking Sheet Pear Tart, *138–139*
barrels, 17
le Bars, Romain, 16
bass (fish)
    Whole Roasted Harvest Fish, *84–85*
beef. *See also* veal
    Boeuf Bourguignon, *104–105*
    Bollito Misto with Pearà Sauce, *204–205*
    Nikujaga with Yuzu Kosho, *72–73*
Beer-Braised Rabbit with Prunes, *52–53*
beets
    Wine Beets and Citrus, *132–133*
Bertaiola, Alessia and Stefano, 200–205
Béru, Athénaïs de, 78–85
Bini, Gabrio, Geneviève and Giotto, 238–245
Blauert, Anne Bruun, 149–155
    Broccolini with Preserved Lemons, *154–155*
    Wild Mushroom Risotto, *152–153*
blouge wines, 26
Boeuf Bourguignon, *104–105*
Bollito Misto with Pearà Sauce, *204–205*
Bouju, Patrick, 126–133
Braised Lamb Shank with Spelt, *130–131*
Bringer, Patrick, 87–91
Broccolini with Preserved Lemons, *154–155*
Burgundy, France, 74–123
    Château de Béru, 78–85
    Domaine Chandon de Briailles, 100–105
    Domaine les Faverelles, 87–91
    Henry, Marthe, 92–99
    Maison en Belles Lies, 106–113
    Maison Valette, 114–123

C

Caillettes, *160–161*
Cantina Marilina (winery), 231–237
    Fried Bread with Eggs, *236–237*
    Zucchini Leaf Soup, *234–235*
capers
    Panelle with Spicy Caper Condiment, *244–245*
carbonic maceration, 17, 26
Carrot Salad with Lentils, Shiso, and Sesame Seeds, *70–71*
casks (vessel), 17
chaptalization, defined, 17
Château de Béru (winery), 24, 78–85
    Whole Roasted Harvest Fish, *84–85*

cheese. *See also specific cheeses by name*
    Bollito Misto with Pearà Sauce, 204–205
    Late Summer Stuffed Garden Vegetables, *168–169*
    Rabbit Biechi, *180–181*
    Tagliatelle with Zucchini and Gorgonzola, *212–213*
    Zucchini Soup with Fresh Cheese, *188–189*
chicken
    Bollito Misto with Pearà Sauce, 204–205
    Gaston Gérard Chicken, *96–97*
    Roast Chicken with Morels and Vin Jaune, *60–61*
clarifying agents, 23
commercial yeast, defined, 19
comté cheese
    Gaston Gérard Chicken, *96–97*
    Mâconnais Onion Soup, *120–121*
    Quiche Lorraine with Wild Mushrooms, *90–91*
condiments
    Apple Mostarda, *204–205*
    Panelle with Spicy Caper Condiment, *244–245*
conventional winemaking
    comparison to natural winemaking, 19–24
    vineyard, 21–22
    wine cellar, 22–23
cooperative (organization), 17
Cornelissen, Frank, 26, 222–229
couscous
    Kabyle Couscous with Lamb, *146–147*
cream and milk
    French Veal Stew, *46–47*
    Gaston Gérard Chicken, *96–97*
    Grandmother's Crème Caramel, *98–99*
    Île Flottante, *122–123*
    Quiche Lorraine with Wild Mushrooms, *90–91*
    Roast Chicken with Morels and Vin Jaune, *60–61*
    Salad with Pea Vinaigrette, *62–63*
    Slow-Cooked Pork with White Wine and Root Vegetables, *110–111*
cru, defined, 17
Cunin, Manu, 156–159
cuvée, defined, 17

D

decolorants, 23
Demeter-certified wines, 21
de Nicolay, François and Claude, 100–105
desserts and sweets
    Baking Sheet Pear Tart, *138–139*
    Fresh Plum Tart, *112–113*
    Grandmother's Crème Caramel, *98–99*
    Île Flottante, *122–123*
Les Deux Terres (winery), 156–159
    Caillettes, *160–161*
disgorgement, defined, 17
DOC, defined, 17
Domaine Chandon de Briailles (winery), 100–105
    Boeuf Bourguignon, *104–105*
Domaine de L'ange Vin (winery), 35, 37–47
    Endive Salad with Boiled Eggs, *44–45*
    French Veal Stew, *46–47*
Domaine des Miroirs (winery), 65–73
    Carrot Salad with Lentils, Shiso, and Sesame Seeds, *70–71*
    Nikujaga with Yuzu Kosho, *72–73*
Domaine la Bohème (winery), 126–133
    Braised Lamb Shank with Spelt, *130–131*
    Wine Beets and Citrus, *132–133*
Domaine les Faverelles (winery), 87–91
    Quiche Lorraine with Wild Mushrooms, *90–91*
Domaine Tessier (winery), 35, 49–53
    Beer-Braised Rabbit with Prunes, *52–53*
dosage, defined, 17

E

eggs
    Endive Salad with Boiled Eggs, *44–45*
    Fried Bread with Eggs, *236–237*
    Grandmother's Crème Caramel, *98–99*
    Île Flottante, *122–123*
    Quiche Lorraine with Wild Mushrooms, *90–91*
eggs (vessels), 17
élevage, defined, 17
Emilia-Romagna, Italy, 191–197
    Sebastian Van De Sype Winery, 192–197
Endive Salad with Boiled Eggs, *44–45*

F

Fargier, Vincent, 156–159
Fenals, Pierre and Michèle, 106–113
fermentation. *See also* yeasts
    conventional, 23
    making natural wine, 21, 24
    secondary fermentation, defined, 18
figs
    Baked Porcini and Fig Salad, *218–219*
filtration, defined, 18
fining agents, 18
fish
    Whole Roasted Harvest Fish, *84–85*
Foradori, Elisabetta, 27, 184–189
France. *See also* French winemakers; French wineries
    Auvergne, 125–139
    Burgundy, 74–123
    history of natural wine, 32–33
    Jura, 55–73
    Languedoc, 163–169
    Loire valley, 35–53
    regions, 30–169
    Rhône valley, 140–161
    wineries, 37–169
French Veal Stew, *46–47*
French winemakers
    Béru, Athénaïs de, 78–85
    Blauert, Anne Bruun, 149–155
    Bouju, Patrick, 126–133
    Bringer, Patrick, 87–91
    Cunin, Manu, 156–159
    Fargier, Vincent, 156–159
    Fenals, Pierre and Michèle, 106–113
    Georgelin, Isabelle, 87–91
    Henry, Marthe, 92–99
    Kagami, Kenjro and Mayumi, 65–73
    Loiseau, Justine, 126–133
    Nicolay, François and Claude de, 100–105
    Robinot, Jean-Pierre and Noëlla, 37–47
    Sénat, Charlotte and Jean-Baptiste, 164–169
    Sene, Lolita, 142–147
    Steen, Anders Frederik, 149–155
    Tessier, Simon and Philippe, 49–53
    Tricot, Marie and Vincent, 134–139
    Valette, Philippe and Cécile, 114–123
    Worobeck, Katie, 56–63

French wineries
    Blauert, Anne Bruun, 149–155
    Château de Béru, 78–85
    Les Deux Terres, 156–159
    Domaine Chandon de Briailles, 100–105
    Domaine de L'ange Vin, 37–47
    Domaine des Miroirs, 65–73
    Domaine la Bohème, 126–133
    Domaine les Faverelles, 87–91
    Domaine Tessier, 49–53
    Henry, Marthe, 92–99
    Maison en Belles Lies, 106–113
    Maison Maenad, 56–63
    Maison Valette, 114–123
    Sénat, Charlotte and Jean-Baptiste, 164–169
    Sene, Lolita, 142–147
    Steen, Anders Frederik, 149–155
    Tricot, Marie and Vincent, 134–139
Fresh Plum Tart, *112–113*
Fried Bread with Eggs, *236–237*
Friuli Venezia Giulia, Italy, 174–181
    Azienda Agricola Dario Prinčič, 175, 176–181
fruit
    Apple Mostarda, *204–205*
    Baked Porcini and Fig Salad, *218–219*
    Baking Sheet Pear Tart, *138–139*
    Beer-Braised Rabbit with Prunes, *52–53*
    Fresh Plum Tart, *112–113*
Fukuoka, Masanobu, 22

G

Gaston Gérard Chicken, *96–97*
Georgelin, Isabelle, 87–91
La Ginestra (winery), 20, 208–213
    Tagliatelle with Zucchini and Gorgonzola, *212–213*
glou-glou red wines, 26
gorgonzola
    Tagliatelle with Zucchini and Gorgonzola, *212–213*
Grana Padano cheese
    Bollito Misto with Pearà Sauce, *204–205*
Grandmother's Crème Caramel, *98–99*
grape leaves
    Baked Porcini and Fig Salad, *218–219*
grape marc
    Whole Roasted Harvest Fish, *84–85*
grape must, defined, 18
grape varietal, defined, 18

H

ham
    Slow-Cooked Pork with White Wine and Root Vegetables, *110–111*
Henry, Marthe, 92–99
    Gaston Gérard Chicken, *96–97*
    Grandmother's Crème Caramel, *98–99*
history of natural wine
    France, 32–33
    Italy, 172–173

I

Île Flottante, *122–123*
indigenous or native grap varietals, 18
indigenous yeast
    defined, 19
    in the vineyard, 21
inoculated yeast, defined, 19
Italian winemakers
    Bertaiola, Alessia and Stefano, 200–205
    Bini, Gabrio, Geneviève and Giotto, 238–245
    Cornelissen, Frank, 222–229
    Foradori, Elisabetta, 184–189
    Nocci, Dario, 208–213
    Paternò, Marilina, 231–237
    Prinčič, Dario, 175, 176–181
    Proietti, Pierluca and Daniele, 216–219
    Rinaldi, Matteo, 208–213
    Van De Sype, Sebastian and Marieke, 192–197
Italian wineries
    Abbia Nòva, 216–219
    Azienda Agricola Dario Prinčič, 175, 176–181
    Azienda Agricola Foradori, 184–189
    Azienda Agricola Frank Cornelissen, 222–229
    Azienda Agricola Serragghia, 238–245
    Cantina Marilina, 231–237
    La Ginestra, 208–213
    Sassara Vini, 200–205
    Sebastian Van De Sype Winery, 192–197

Italy. *See also* Italian winemakers; Italian wineries
    Emilia-Romagna, 191–197
    Friuli Venezia Giulia, 174–181
    history of natural wine, 172–173
    Lazio, 215–219
    regions, 171–244
    Sicily, 220–245
    Trentino-Alto Adige, 183–189
    Tuscany, 206–213
    Veneto, 199–205
    wineries, 176–245

J

Jura, France, 55–73
    Domaine des Miroirs, 65–73
    Maison Maenad, 56–63

K

Kabyle Couscous with Lamb, *146–147*
Kagami, Kenjro and Mayumi, 65–73

L

labneh
    Zucchini Soup with Fresh Cheese, *188–189*
lamb
    Braised Lamb Shank with Spelt, *130–131*
    Kabyle Couscous with Lamb, *146–147*
Languedoc, France, 163–169
    Sénat, Charlotte and Jean-Baptiste, 164–169
Late Summer Stuffed Garden Vegetables, *168–169*
Lazio, Italy, 215–219
    Abbia Nòva, 216–219
lees
    defined, 18
    in natural winemaking, 24
lentils
    Carrot Salad with Lentils, Shiso, and Sesame Seeds, *70–71*
Loire valley, France, 35–53
    Domaine de L'ange Vin, 35, 37–47
    Domaine Tessier, 35, 49–53
Loiseau, Justine, 126–133

M

maceration, 17, 18
Mâconnais Onion Soup, *120–121*
Maison en Belles Lies (winery), 106–113
    Fresh Plum Tart, *112–113*
    Slow-Cooked Pork with White Wine and Root Vegetables, *110–111*
Maison Maenad (winery), 19, 56–63
    Roast Chicken with Morels and Vin Jaune, *60–61*
    Salad with Pea Vinaigrette, *62–63*
Maison Valette (winery), 24, 114–123
    Île Flottante, *122–123*
    Mâconnais Onion Soup, *120–121*
Meursault, France, 92–99
milk. *See* cream and milk
minerality, defined, 18
morel mushrooms
    Roast Chicken with Morels and Vin Jaune, *60–61*
    Wild Mushroom Risotto, *152–153*
mouse (tasting term), defined, 18
mushrooms
    Baked Porcini and Fig Salad, *218–219*
    Boeuf Bourguignon, *104–105*
    French Veal Stew, *46–47*
    Quiche Lorraine with Wild Mushrooms, *90–91*
    Roast Chicken with Morels and Vin Jaune, *60–61*
    Wild Mushroom Risotto, *152–153*

N

native grape varietals, 18
native yeasts
    defined, 19
    in the vineyard, 21
natural wines and winemaking. *See also* history of natural wine
    comparison to conventional, 19–24
    history of natural wine, 32–33, 172–173
    overview, 19–24
    shades and styles of, 25–27
    vineyard, 22
    wine cellar, 24
négociants, defined, 18
Nikujaga with Yuzu Kosho, *72–73*
Nocci, Dario, 208–213

O

oak tannins, 23
onions
    Beer-Braised Rabbit with Prunes, *52–53*
    Boeuf Bourguignon, *104–105*
    Bollito Misto with Pearà Sauce, *204–205*
    Braised Lamb Shank with Spelt, *130–131*
    French Veal Stew, *46–47*
    Kabyle Couscous with Lamb, *146–147*
    Mâconnais Onion Soup, *120–121*
    Nikujaga with Yuzu Kosho, *72–73*
    Osso Bucco, *196–197*
    Rabbit Biechi, *180–181*
    Slow-Cooked Pork with White Wine and Root Vegetables, *110–111*
    Tagliatelle with Zucchini and Gorgonzola, *212–213*
    Wild Mushroom Risotto, *152–153*
    Zucchini Leaf Soup, *234–235*
    Zucchini Soup with Fresh Cheese, *188–189*
orange or skin-contact wine, 25–26
organic farming certifications, 22
organic wines, 21
organoleptic, defined, 18
Osso Bucco, *196–197*
oxidation, defined, 18

P

Panelle with Spicy Caper Condiment, *244–245*
Parmigiano Reggiano
    Late Summer Stuffed Garden Vegetables, *168–169*
    Rabbit Biechi, *180–181*
    Wild Mushroom Risotto, *152–153*
pasta
    Rabbit Biechi, *180–181*
    Tagliatelle with Zucchini and Gorgonzola, *212–213*
    Zucchini Leaf Soup, *234–235*
Paternò, Marilina, 231–237
paysan, defined, 18
pearà sauce
    Bollito Misto with Pearà Sauce, *204–205*
pears
    Baking Sheet Pear Tart, *138–139*

peas
    Salad with Pea Vinaigrette, *62–63*
pét-nat (pétillant naturel) wine, 25
plums
    Fresh Plum Tart, *112–113*
pomace
    Whole Roasted Harvest Fish, *84–85*
porcini mushrooms
    Baked Porcini and Fig Salad, *218–219*
pork. *See also* bacon
    Caillettes, *160–161*
    Late Summer Stuffed Garden Vegetables, *168–169*
    Slow-Cooked Pork with White Wine and Root Vegetables, *110–111*
Prinčič, Dario, 26, 175, 176–181
Proietti, Pierluca and Daniele, 216–219
prunes
    Beer-Braised Rabbit with Prunes, *52–53*

Q

Quiche Lorraine with Wild Mushrooms, *90–91*

R

rabbit
    Beer-Braised Rabbit with Prunes, *52–53*
    Rabbit Biechi, *180–181*
rares (wines), defined, 18
reduction (tasting term), defined, 18
red wines, 23 fig., 26–27
regions
    Auvergne, France, 125–139
    Burgundy, France, 74–123
    Emilia-Romagna, Italy, 191–197
    France, 30–169
    Friuli Venezia Giulia, Italy, 174–181
    Italy, 171–244
    Jura, France, 55–73
    Languedoc, France, 163–169
    Lazio, Italy, 215–219
    Loire valley, France, 35–53
    Rhône valley, France, 140–161
    Sicily, Italy, 220–245
    Trentino-Alto Adige, Italy, 183–189
    Tuscany, Italy, 206–213
    Veneto, Italy, 199–205
residual sugar, defined, 18

Rhône valley, France, 140–161
  Blauert, Anne Bruun, 149–155
  Les Deux Terres, 156–159
  Sene, Lolita, 142–147
  Steen, Anders Frederik, 149–155
rice
  Wild Mushroom Risotto, *152–153*
Rinaldi, Matteo, 208–213
Roast Chicken with Morels and Vin Jaune, *60–61*
Robinot, Jean-Pierre and Noëlla, 37–47
robust red wines, 26–27
root vegetables
  Beer-Braised Rabbit with Prunes, *52–53*
  Braised Lamb Shank with Spelt, *130–131*
  Carrot Salad with Lentils, Shiso, and Sesame Seeds, *70–71*
  French Veal Stew, *46–47*
  Kabyle Couscous with Lamb, *146–147*
  Late Summer Stuffed Garden Vegetables, *168–169*
  Nikujaga with Yuzu Kosho, *72–73*
  Slow-Cooked Pork with White Wine and Root Vegetables, *110–111*
  Wine Beets and Citrus, *132–133*
rosé wines, 26

S

salads
  Baked Porcini and Fig Salad, *218–219*
  Carrot Salad with Lentils, Shiso, and Sesame Seeds, *70–71*
  Endive Salad with Boiled Eggs, *44–45*
  Salad with Pea Vinaigrette, *62–63*
Sassara Vini (winery), 200–205
  Bollito Misto with Peará Sauce, *204–205*
sausage
  Bollito Misto with Peará Sauce, *204–205*
Sebastian Van De Sype Winery, 192–197
  Osso Bucco, *196–197*
secondary fermentation
  defined, 18
  pét-nat (pétillant naturel) wine, 25
selective yeast, defined, 19
Sénat, Charlotte and Jean-Baptiste, 164–169
  Late Summer Stuffed Garden Vegetables, *168–169*
Sene, Lolita, 142–147
  Kabyle Couscous with Lamb, *146–147*
shiso
  Carrot Salad with Lentils, Shiso, and Sesame Seeds, *70–71*
Sicily, Italy, 220–245
  Azienda Agricola Frank Cornelissen, 26, 222–229
  Azienda Agricola Serragghia, 238–245
  Cantina Marilina, 231–237
skin-contact white wine, 25–26
Slow-Cooked Pork with White Wine and Root Vegetables, *110–111*
soups and stews
  Boeuf Bourguignon, *104–105*
  French Veal Stew, *46–47*
  Mâconnais Onion Soup, *120–121*
  Nikujaga with Yuzu Kosho, *72–73*
  Zucchini Leaf Soup, *234–235*
  Zucchini Soup with Fresh Cheese, *188–189*
sparkling wine
  pét-nat wine, 25
spelt
  Braised Lamb Shank with Spelt, *130–131*
Steen, Anders Frederik, 149–155
  Broccolini with Preserved Lemons, *154–155*
  Wild Mushroom Risotto, *152–153*
Steiner, Rudolf, 22
sterilization, effect on fermentation, 23
stews. *See* soups and stews
sulfites (sulfur dioxide or SO_2)
  defined, 18
  in natural wine production, 24
sweet wines, 27
swish chard
  Baked Porcini and Fig Salad, *218–219*
  Caillettes, *160–161*

T

Tagliatelle with Zucchini and Gorgonzola, *212–213*
tanks (vessel), defined, 18
tannins
  conventional winemaking and, 23
  defined, 18
Tempura Artichoke Hearts, *228–229*
terroir
  defined, 18
  loss in conventional winemaking, 23
  in natural wine production, 24
Tessier, Simon and Philippe, 49–53
tomatoes
  Late Summer Stuffed Garden Vegetables, *168–169*
  Zucchini Leaf Soup, *234–235*
Trentino-Alto Adige, Italy, 183–189
  Azienda Agricola Foradori (winery), 26, 184–189
Tricot, Marie and Vincent, 134–139
  Baking Sheet Pear Tart, *138–139*
Tuscany, Italy, 206–213
  La Ginestra (winery), 208–213

V

Valette, Philippe and Cécile, 114–123
Van De Sype, Sebastian and Marieke, 192–197
veal
  Bollito Misto with Peará Sauce, *204–205*
  French Veal Stew, *46–47*
  Osso Bucco, *196–197*
vegetables. *See also* root vegetables; salads; *specific vegetables by name*
  Bollito Misto with Peará Sauce, *204–205*
  Caillettes, *160–161*
  Late Summer Stuffed Garden Vegetables, *168–169*
  Mâconnais Onion Soup, *120–121*
  Osso Bucco, *196–197*
  Salad with Pea Vinaigrette, *62–63*
  Tempura Artichoke Hearts, *228–229*
  Wine Beets and Citrus, *132–133*
  Zucchini Leaf Soup, *234–235*
  Zucchini Soup with Fresh Cheese, *188–189*
Veneto, Italy, 199–205
  Sassara Vini (winery), 200–205
vigneron, defined, 18
vineyard operations
  conventional, 21–22
  natural, 22
vintage, defined, 18
volatile acidity, defined, 19

W

white wines, 24 fig., 25–26

Whole Roasted Harvest Fish, *84–85*
Wild Mushroom Risotto, *152–153*
wild yeasts
    defined, 19
    in the vineyard, 21
Wine Beets and Citrus, *132–133*
wine cellar operations
    conventional, 22–23
    natural, 24
wineries
    Abbia Nòva, Italy, 216–219
    Azienda Agricola Dario Prinčič, Italy, 175, 176–181
    Azienda Agricola Foradori, Italy, 184–189
    Azienda Agricola Frank Cornelissen, Italy, 222–229
    Azienda Agricola Serragghia, Italy, 238–245
    Blauert, Anne Bruun, France, 149–155
    Cantina Marilina, Italy, 231–237
    Château de Béru, France, 78–85
    Les Deux Terres, France, 156–159
    Domaine Chandon de Briailles, France, 100–105
    Domaine de L'ange Vin, France, 37–47
    Domaine des Miroirs, France, 65–73
    Domaine la Bohème, France, 126–133
    Domaine les Faverelles, France, 87–91
    Domaine Tessier, France, 49–53
    France, 37–169
    La Ginestra, Italy, 208–213
    Henry, Marthe, France, 92–99
    Italy, 176–245
    Maison en Belles Lies, France, 106–113
    Maison Maenad, France, 56–63
    Maison Valette, France, 114–123
    Sassara Vini, Italy, 200–205
    Sebastian Van De Sype Winery, Italy, 192–197
    Sénat, Charlotte and Jean-Baptiste, France, 164–169
    Sene, Lolita, France, 142–147
    Steen, Anders Frederik, France, 149–155
    Tricot, Marie and Vincent, France, 134–139
Worobeck, Katie, 56–63

Y

yeasts
    defined, 19
    natural winemaking, 21, 24

Z

zero-zero wines, defined, 19
zucchini
    Tagliatelle with Zucchini and Gorgonzola, *212–213*
    Zucchini Leaf Soup, *234–235*
    Zucchini Soup with Fresh Cheese, *188–189*

First published in the United States of America in 2025 by
Rizzoli International Publications, Inc.
300 Park Avenue South
New York, NY 10010
www.rizzoliusa.com

Copyright © Stephanie Mercier Voyer, Zev Rovine, David McMillan, Xavier Tera

Publisher: Charles Miers
Editor: Ellen Nidy
Design: Brian Roettinger (Perron-Roettinger)
Production Manager: Rebecca Ambrose
Managing Editor: Lynn Scrabis

All rights reserved. No part of this publication may be reproduced, stored in a retrieval system, or transmitted in any form or by any means, electronic, mechanical, photocopying, recording, or otherwise, without prior consent of the publishers.

Printed in China

2025 2026 2027 2028 / 10 9 8 7 6 5 4 3 2 1

ISBN: 978-0-8478-4400-5
Library of Congress Control Number: 2024861031

Visit us online:
Facebook.com / RizzoliNewYork
instagram.com/rizzolibooks
twitter.com/Rizzoli_Books
pinterest.com/rizzolibooks
youtube.com/user/RizzoliNY
issuu.com/rizzoli